To Chris I pray that this book will inspire you to reach the dreams that God has placed within you. Know that your life has purpose and I am confident that you will live within that purpose and be very successful.

God Ble.

To Chris I pray that this book will inspire you to reach the dreams that God has placed within you. Know that your life has purpose and I am confident that you will live within that purpose and be very successful.

God Bless

Living For Friday Dreading Sunday Night

A Five Day Voyage to the Shores of Your Destiny

ERIC MOORE

Copyright © 2012 by Eric Moore
Scriptures noted NKJV are taken from the New King James Version.
Thomas Nelson, Inc., Publishers.

ISBN 978-0-7414-7610-4

Printed in the United States of America

Published May 2013

INFINITY PUBLISHING
1094 New DeHaven Street, Suite 100
West Conshohocken, PA 19428-2713
Toll-free (877) BUY BOOK
Local Phone (610) 941-9999
Fax (610) 941-9959
Info@buybooksontheweb.com
www.buybooksontheweb.com

This book is dedicated to my grandfather Willie Moore (1919-2004). You were the person who showed me by example what it takes to truly live life as a servant of God. I am eternally grateful for the wisdom, knowledge and understanding that you imparted into my life.

To my mother Marva, my biggest supporter throughout my life, I thank you for pushing me whenever I didn't feel like moving. The encouragement you have given me and sacrifices you made on my behalf are appreciated beyond the significant measure of any words I could use to describe my gratitude. To my late father Jack Taylor Jr., thank you for sharpening my mind and contributing to the shaping of my intellect. To my grandmother Mary, and the rest of my immediate and extended family, I thank each of you for your support and unwavering love during my lifetime.

Lastly this book is dedicated to the readers of it, who have decided that up to this point their life's potential has outweighed their life's production. That their dreams long imagined are now worthy of being transformed into their future reality.

Acknowledgements

I would like to thank the individuals who have helped sow seeds of encouragement into my life both previously and during the writing process of this book. You have encouraged me both up close and at a distance. Through the examples of your lives each of you have provided me with immeasurable levels of inspiration.

Kien Hunter	Jennifer Slayden
Kevin Smith	Brennen Bryant
James Morton	Ty Armour
Donnell Patrick	Barbara Brooks
David Trotter	Vickie Sosebee
Derrick Barker	Shanti Johnson
Quentin Harris	Jocqueus Wilson
Billy Johnson	Dontez Hunter
Johnny Robinson	Oprah Winfrey
Les Brown	Delatorro McNeal II

Elder Willie B. Jackson and the Redeem COGIC
Pastor Kevin Adams and the Olivet Baptist Church
Dr.Charles Adams and the HMBC
Dr.Freddie Haynes and the FWBC
Pastor Joel Osteen and the Lakewood Church

Contents

Introduction

God has always been very good to me in my life. I have a wonderful family, great friends, and the ability to eat and live within a climate controlled environment. At twenty-six years old, I was at the point in my life where I wanted to know that my life was taking the right direction. I had within me a burning desire to make a tangible contribution to society but I was unsure how to channel it. There was a hunger to be free from my mundane existence. Quite simply, I was sick and tired of living for Friday and dreading Sunday night.

The reason that I did this was due to the fact that I did not like, nor was I passionate about the way I made my living. Don't get me wrong, I worked hard at my job, but I did not have a passion for it. Most days I felt like a robot that was programmed. I had been doing the work for so long that it felt as if I was constantly in auto pilot mode. There was no way that I could have been alone in my feelings especially looking at my co-workers and hearing the stories of people around the country. Just taking one look at the differing energy levels of workers early on a Monday morning compared to a Friday night at close exemplifies my point.

The world is changing swiftly and the time has come for America to arise and awaken from its slumber. There is a shift in culture happening, as we transition from the industrial age into the age of information. A 20th century mentality will hinder us from reaching our full God given potential in a 21st century society. Many of us have gone through life with a sense of entitlement, allowing a mentality of mediocrity to ascertain the hallmarks of success.

These methods of thinking must be eliminated if we are to become all that God has created us to be within the 21st century. The inconvenient truth is the world owes us nothing. It does however provide each of us with the opportunity to prove that we belong here. We can each become successful here with the application of the gifts and talents that God placed within us. For when we refine them and apply them, their strength propels us into a life of greatness.

A lifestyle of greatness is first birthed within our minds. None of us is great at all things, but each of us has the capability to be great at something positive. Far too many individuals have let allergic reactions to education open the floodgates of chronic failure and missed opportunities. This has resulted in the delay or denial of God's destiny for many of us. God did not create us and send us to earth to work, pay bills, and then die. God created each of us on purpose, to live lives filled with purpose and a defined destiny. Each of us must choose to become the masters of our own destiny.

To become all that God has called us to be, we must obtain and apply knowledge in five different forms. The first type of knowledge is spiritual knowledge. This type of knowledge encourages us to possess a real relationship with God and understand the knowledge of his power and greatness. The second type of knowledge we must obtain is academic knowledge. It benefits us by providing us with the ability to earn a living and function within the framework of society.

The third type of knowledge we must obtain is life knowledge. It is gleaned through our personal experiences and the life experiences of the individuals we observe and/or admire. It also includes the very important variable known as common sense. The fourth type of knowledge that we must obtain is field knowledge. This knowledge is gained through learning our desired work fields inside and out. This type of knowledge will help us to become the best workers we can be within our chosen vocation. The fifth type of knowledge is financial knowledge. Each of us must learn to become proficient in handling our finances, because after all they are our finances.

Recent history has given us scores of examples as to why the government and many so-called financial experts may not have our best interests in mind, in terms of our individual financial pictures. When we combine these five different types of knowledge, it equips each of us with the tools to become all that God has destined us to be within the 21st century.

The fact that you are reading this book is not an accident or a circumstance generated by luck. It was written with the purpose to give hope and improve the lives of all who read it. There are too many people on earth and within the United States of America more specifically, who have had destinies delayed or denied all together. It is the aim of this book to change destinies delayed or denied, into destinies expedited and fulfilled.

I am not foolish enough to believe that I have all the answers for every life situation, but I am wise enough to know where to direct the questions that I lack the answers to. What I have to offer however, are several solutions to facilitate the quality of life improvement and destiny fulfillment that many of us seek to attain during our time on this earth. This book will encourage and motivate anyone who reads it to conduct self-examination of their lives, and create and execute a plan to reach God's destiny for them. There is something for everyone contained within the pages of this book. In the same breath however, it is important to remember that not everything contained within these pages is meant for everyone.

Many of us have lived our lives far too long living on the weekend, and existing during the week. The time has come for us to start living every day and enjoying our differing journeys through life. In the 21st century greatness is no longer optional, but a prerequisite to successfully reaching your destiny.

I implore you to use this book as a tool to help facilitate your pathway to destiny. Allow its messages to inspire you and help take your life to heights previously thought to be unattainable. Let it challenge you to reclaim the dreams in your heart and resuscitate them. Take what you need from it and let it challenge you to become the best person that God has created you to be.

PART ONE

Monday

THE NEED FOR TRANSITION

CHAPTER 1

The Urgent Call Of Greatness

Many Sundays in my life I have walked into church feeling disillusioned and dejected. Amazingly after a couple of hours of praise and worship my whole outlook would change. I would feel renewed and energized, ready to take on and conquer any challenge the world presented to me. The great feelings would follow me all through my day up until Monday morning, when my alarm clock would go off waking me up for work.

You may or may not go to church on a Sunday morning that is just my personal example. Your sense of escape from the daily grind could be a weeklong vacation, or a weekend getaway. Unfortunately, others of us may have found our short term breakaway at the bottom of a liquor bottle or at the high point of an illicit drug. No matter what our means of escapism consists of, we all must face the alarm clock chimes on Monday morning.

The alarm clock represents the call of our reality. We cannot escape our realities, but each of us has the means to make them work out in our favor. We have to find a way to take our positive escapes such as church, or vacation and make our realities equally as enjoyable. Far too many of us fall into a deep cauldron of trouble, simply because we cannot stand to face the realities of life. Our dreams have the ability to become our realities if we learn to properly channel our energy and be hungry for them.

We are all dealt different hands in this life, but those who succeed learn to play any hand to their advantage. When we delve into the cruel and unforgiving clutches of drug abuse, excessive alcohol consumption, and other chronically negative behaviors we throw in our hands. It is important that we keep playing our hands until the game is over. God is the only one with the power to end the game and he knows the cards that we all hold, since he is the entity responsible for dealing them. If he had no plans for us succeeding, he would not have invited us to the table of life to begin with.

When we cheat and try to take a peak at the hands of others, many of us may feel upset and disgusted that their hands may appear to be better than ours. We have to remember that all it takes is one card, (a touch of God's grace) to turn any situation around in our favor. God's blessings and gifts for someone else are for them only. When we keep our focus on our cards, and play them to the best of our abilities, everything will take care of itself. There are no losers in this game, for God created and destined each and every single one of us to win. He loves us too much and paid far too high a price on the cross for us to then disrespect him by claiming what he placed within us is insufficient. Every one in this world means something to someone. There is no such thing as an insignificant person.

Life is similar to a big Hollywood production. The director (God) has roles designed specifically for each and every one of us. Not everyone is meant to be a big star in the eyes of the world, but there can never be enough best supporting actors or crew members. When we do all of our jobs to the best of our abilities, we truly make the production great. You can be good in any area of life that you choose to partake in. You will be great in the area of life that God chooses you to partake in. That is where you can be a star within his Kingdom. You are the best at something you just may have not tapped into yet. When you finally discover and pursue what you are great at, that is when money will chase you instead of the other way around. A lot of people are good at many different things and for one reason or another

4

never discover what they are truly great at. At some point the decision must be made to stop jogging from your dreams and start sprinting toward your destiny. This book will propel your sprint.

Below I have listed several examples of individuals who have used their gifts and talents to operate in the realm of greatness.

Michael Jordan playing basketball
Usain Bolt sprinting on a track
Jerry Rice catching a football
Tiger Woods hitting a golf ball
Martin Luther King leading non-violent protests
Barbara Walters conducting an interview
Warren Buffett negotiating a business deals
Michael Jackson singing and dancing

The individuals that I listed above all were able to take the gifts and talents that God gave them and each maximized their abilities. For them it was simply not good enough for them to just rest on their natural ability alone. Each and every one of them put in the time, dedication and sacrifice that was necessary to master their God chosen crafts. You can look at each and every one of them and use the phrase that God put each and every one of them on this earth to touch the world with their gifts. These individuals were not only able to use what God gave them, but managed to nurture, enhance and grow their gifts through diligent work. They were essentially going after God, by maximizing the potential of their gifts. They did not look around hoping and waiting for miracles to happen. They all had the keen insight and ability to realize that the miracle was already placed inside of them from birth.

Millions of people are living their lives at less than half their potential, because they look around and see a lot of other people doing the same. If you are one of those people it is time to wake up and realize that good enough is not good enough any longer. The time has come for greatness to overtake the place of goodness and mediocrity within this life. Natural ability matched with minimal or non-existent work ethic equals wasted potential.

Regular Versus Premium

So many people are living and settling for regular unleaded lives without reaching their premium potential. As human beings our tanks are represented by our actions, which are fueled by our thoughts. What are you filling up your life on? You may say Eric, it costs a lot more to fill up with premium potential and I only know and can afford a regular unleaded life. This is not true due to the fact that God designed each of us similarly to high performance sports cars. If you look at the owner's manual of a high performance sports car, it specifies that the vehicle requires premium fuel only to function properly. This is because the vehicle was built with such meticulous care and design, that only the best grade of gasoline is sufficient for it.

Have you ever tried putting regular gasoline in a vehicle that was designated premium only? The result will be an engine filled with gunk, and may cause the engine severe problems. The improper gasoline will also rob the vehicle of its ability to achieve its maximum capable performance. Some auto companies may even decide to void your warranty for filling up with improper fuel. The improper fuel throws off the timing of the pistons in the engine, thus leading to the eventual destruction of the engine.

The same things that can happen to a high performance vehicle can happen to each and every one of us that continues to let regular unleaded thinking fill our minds. We are all created by God to live high performance premium lives. This type of life is birthed within our thoughts and is manifested through the output of our actions.

Regular unleaded living is spawned from negative thoughts such as the ones listed below.

- God does not love me
- I can't succeed
- My situation will never improve
- No one cares about me
- My life is insignificant
- I have no reason to try
- I have tried before and failed
- Rules and Consequences don't apply to me

Examples of regular unleaded living are listed below.

- Lack of a spiritual foundation
- Depression
- Drug Abuse
- Alcohol Abuse
- Unhealthy Addictions
- Dishonesty with yourself and/or others
- Disrespecting others
- Allowing yourself to be disrespected by others
- Giving less than your best effort in any task that you have committed to
- Never learning to be comfortable in your own skin

All of the aforementioned behaviors in their own ways have contributed to millions of people living regular unleaded lives. Everyone including me at times deal with regular unleaded thoughts and/or actions. They lead to us getting down on ourselves. When this happens it is imperative that you do not stay down, because you cannot reach your destiny if you quit on your journey. Quitting is easy, but truly living is hard to do.

We are all equipped with everything we need to live the life that God has destined for us. There is no need to study the horoscopes or go for weekly visits to the local psychic. The crystal ball we seek is self-contained. It is represented in the form of our visions and dreams for our lives. These are revealed to us when we take the time to ask God to reveal his plans for our lives with us through earnest prayer time and meditation. We may not get the answer we want, or the timing we seek, but rest assure that the correct answer will come just in time.

I wanted to write this book at least five years ago, but it simply was not the right time. There were things that God needed to reveal to me to truly make the work powerful. People asked me for years when I would write a book that would help people, but I sheepishly had no answers for them. I grew frustrated and became mired in currents of regular unleaded thoughts and actions. I was unfocused and swimming in swift currents of desolation and depression in the sea of mediocrity.

I prayed that God would bail me out by sending me a life raft (my purpose for living). It took several years for me to figure out that the life raft he sent for me wasn't going to drop out of the sky for me to easily reach out and grab it. I had to learn to swim in the direction of where he placed the raft. The seas were rough, and there were many days when I was unsure if I would make it to my life raft. I didn't think I could swim that well, but you are capable of much more than you realize once you are in the fight for your dreams. It took years but now I have finally reached my life raft.

He never abandoned me even when I felt most alone. There were nights when I wondered whether he cared about me or was too busy helping other people to hear my prayers and cries. He never left me through it all. At the time I didn't realize that he needed me to learn and grow on my own. It would have been far too easy for him to just give me the life raft when I requested it, but looking back, it wouldn't have benefited me in the least bit.

I needed to learn to have faith and understand that the help that I requested was sent for me to uncover. I swam for years doing all the dirty work (research, prayer, living right and helping others) while hunting for my raft. Just when I felt that my strength was waning my raft appeared. For years I watched people around me finding their life rafts and I wondered if mine had gone and sailed away. I finally reached it and I hope this book will help many of you stay strong while swimming toward your raft. My time spent swimming through the sea of mediocrity prepared me for my destiny (the place where our purpose is applied daily) by helping me build character and grow both mentally and spiritually.

Land of Security

The problem that many of us have is that we never leave the land of security and non-risk to pursue our destiny. For most of us we are taught to play life safe and to avoid taking risks. According to noted author and businessman Robert Kiyosaki, "Many people's idea of normal is to play it safe by climbing the corporate ladder." The problem with climbing the ladder is that there are only a select few that make it to the top and those on top want to stay in their positions of power for as long as possible.

No matter what your skills and qualifications are, it becomes both a waiting game and a political one. It most often is a political game predicated on who you know, as opposed to what you know that helps determine your level of success. This element is greatest in the corporate world. The powers that be in many of these organizations do not want you to improve your skills, because if you do they feel threatened that you may set your sights on their high level positions.

If the corporate world is where God has led you, do all you can to improve yourself regardless of the political landscape at the office. Do not worry about what the powers that be say, improve yourself and make your talents undeniable. The truth is you never know who has their eyes fixed on you and your performance. Your blessing and promotion may not come from the company you are within; it may be from a competitor. Just remember to take God and your knowledge wherever you go.

Not everyone is destined to be a corporate worker, many of us have been destined to go into business for ourselves, work in government, or small business capacities. The problem is that once people reach adulthood, they let others drill into their heads the importance of job security and playing things safe. They throw their dreams out the window and settle into a life in the land of security and non-risk, with shoreline views of the sea of mediocrity. They sacrifice their ability to think outside the box, because it's not seen as the popular way of traversing through adulthood. My friends it is human nature to want to fit in and belong somewhere, but it benefits us only if we are growing and making progress toward our destiny.

The first place where we learn to fit in is at school as young children. No child wants to be ostracized and seen as different and not belonging. We learn early as children to assimilate and conform to the uniformities of our schoolmates. Children are taught and expected to learn inside the box of a one size fits all educational system. Everyone is taught with the intent to make these future adults conform to the requirements of the working class system of life.

If you think about it, the work world is essentially a school without grades. We receive paychecks instead of grades to validate our efforts. Instead of homework, we work overtime. Our school systems are setup to produce workers either blue, white, or black collar. Black collar workers are the blue and white-collar workers who work so much that it changes the color of their collars to black.

The point is our school systems are not designed to produce entrepreneurs, and individuals with dreams and ideas that expand outside of the box referred to as normalcy. In this great country that I love, school children are not encouraged or taught to critically think. For many of us once we reached the working world as adults, our ability to critically think had been suppressed for so long, that all we knew was the inside the box way of life. We then became workers in occupations that were mechanically robotic, and made boredom our best friends.

Soon many of us became trapped behind walls of dreamlessness. We settled for lives tethered to the land of security and non-risk on the shores of the sea of mediocrity. Then we became life partners with compromise and complacency, forgetting about the gifts and talents that God placed within each of us. My friend's complacency is the predator of dreams and compromise is its assistant. In the next chapter I will explore why it is critical that you vacate the land of security and non-risk, and swim toward the shores of your destiny.

Chapter 1 Questions

1. Do I live for Friday and dread Sunday night and if so why?

_____

_____

_____

_____

2. Am I living a regular unleaded life or am I striving to reach my premium potential?

_____

_____

_____

_____

3. What would it take for me to reach my premium potential?

_____

_____

_____

_____

4. What is it that I wish I could do for a living?

_____

_____

_____

_____

5. What is preventing me from doing what my heart knows I should be doing for a living?

_____

_____

_____

_____

Chapter 2

Is Life Within The Box Flawed?

For most of our lives we were taught to work hard, go to school and then get a good job. This philosophy was the standard line given to millions of Americans in the 20th century. Many of us felt that the American dream consisted of going to school, graduating, and landing a good paying job. We were then expected to purchase a house with a 30-year mortgage, while working in our various occupations for that same amount of time. We were then told that after those 30 years, we would be rewarded with retirement, a steady pension, social security, and the ability to finally live life on our terms. By that time, most of our homes would be paid off and we would be empty nesters free to enjoy our retirement years.

I hate to be the bearer of bad news, but that way of life in this country has passed away. America for millions of us has become the land of spoiled milk and stale honey. Outsourcing, corruption and corporate greed have brought our country's financial markets to its knees. This has resulted in an overwhelmingly large number of families dropping off the rolls of the middle class and into the rungs of unmitigated poverty.

This has caused a widening gap between the individuals who have a surplus of money and those who lack it. The middle class who for decades stood as the backbone of our economy has shrunk to unprecedentedly low levels. As of 2012, unemployment levels have reached record numbers all over this great nation. Able-bodied men and women have been forced to use up their personal savings and even rely on government assistance to get by. A by-product of these problems has been a rash of incidents involving good hardworking people under normal circumstances, turning to criminal and immoral activities just to maintain their existence. These individuals are not looking for handouts, but simply the opportunity to support their families.

These circumstances have arguably affected no other region in the nation harder than the state of Michigan and more specifically my hometown of Detroit. Detroit for the majority of the 20th century was the automobile manufacturing capital of the world. It was seen as the sterling foundation of middle-class America. Hardworking and determined Americans such as my grandfather flocked there to work in its once booming automobile industry.

This was a way of life that stretched across generations, races and religious circles. Ford, Chrysler, and General Motors were the model corporate machines in the eyes of many. They employed both blue and white-collar workers not to mention the parts suppliers that relied on their contracts. There was plenty of work to go around, and if a person knew someone within the companies, it almost assured their future chance at being hired. The workers relied on the companies for their healthcare coverage, paychecks, and retirement plans.

End of American Industrial Age

Things began to change when the higher up executives at the auto companies realized that they could save money by outsourcing their production of vehicles to places like Mexico and Southeast Asia. This process was aided in part by the North American Free Trade Agreement (NAFTA) signed into law by President Bill Clinton in 1993. Since paying American workers was much more expensive than paying Mexican or Asian workers, it resulted in record profit increases for the companies at the time. This resulted in the companies being strengthened and the value of the American worker being diminished. The big three did not however count on the quality of their American sold but foreign produced vehicles suffering. This development gave their products a bad reputation in the minds of a large cross section of Americans.

As time passed, a by-product of the perceived lack of vehicle quality opened the door for foreign automakers such as Toyota, Honda and Nissan to capture a large segment of the American auto market. These foreign automakers then took the step of setting up operations within the United States primarily in the southern states of Kentucky, Tennessee, Alabama and South Carolina. These actions by the foreign automakers drove a noticeable wedge into the profits of the big three, causing declines in their sales numbers. As a result, the big three let many of their workers go in the form of massive layoffs and position eliminations.

A large number of people who had given their entire working lives to the companies were all of a sudden on the street trying to find work. By the early 21st century, the American automakers began to struggle mightily under the weight of high fuel prices, foreign competition and rising benefit costs for their employees and retirees.

This was a situation primarily isolated to the auto industry until corporations from other industries saw the profits that outsourcing generated and followed suit by sending manufacturing jobs beyond the borders of our nation. Outsourcing however has not been the only culprit behind the country's economic problems in the early 21st century. There are two more major elements that enabled the rich to get richer and the poor and middle class to get poorer.

Follow The Money Trail

International bankers have also made a strong contribution to the widening gap between social classes. In

1999, President Bill Clinton signed into the law the Gramm-Leach-Bliley Act. The bill was named after its congressional Republican authors, Senator Phil Gramm of Texas, Representative Jim Leach of Iowa and Representative Thomas Bliley of Virginia. The bill allowed for the merger of commercial and investment banks. It also repealed a portion of the Glass-Steagall Act of 1933 which was initially put in place to regulate the banking industry. This piece of legislation opened a Pandora's box of greed and heartless capitalism that many Americans are suffering the effects from today.

Empowered by the Gramm-Leach-Bliley Act, banks began to place risky bets on exotic financial instruments while using the money that was entrusted to them by their depositors. Wall Street essentially became a high stakes casino with the hard earned money of everyday Americans being used to gamble with. Even though outsourcing and bank deregulation helped to bring on the economic issues we have faced in the last five years, there was a third element that greatly accelerated our economic spiral.

The third element that severely hurt our economy was the rise in fuel prices and its domino effect on small businesses and consumers. This element was aided by speculators on Wall Street manipulating the price of oil. It is the goal of speculators to trade barrels of oil on commodities markets which drive up its price and allows them to make substantial short term profits. This was permitted due to soft regulations on energy trading. The regulations were softened in December 2000 when President Bill Clinton signed the Commodity Futures Modernization Act of 2000. This bill contained a section called the Enron Loophole written by Senator Phil Gramm that allowed various energy products exemption from the Commodity Exchange Act of 1936. This act was originally put in place to regulate oil speculation. Now instead of supply and demand having the greatest effect on oil and gas prices, market speculation replaced it. With the law now on their side, all the energy companies and Wall Street speculators needed was a reason to inflate prices.

No Longer Business as Usual

In 2003, our military under the direction of former President George W. Bush, invaded the country of Iraq. This move caused oil prices to spike all over the world, and fuel prices to rise in the (U.S.). Many of the massive numbers of job cuts in this country from the years 2003-2011 are rooted in the meteoric rise in the prices of both oil and gasoline from 2003 forward.

According to the Lundberg survey, the average cost of a regular gallon of gasoline in January 2003 was $1.60 per gallon. This was a full two months before the invasion of Iraq in March of that year. By July 2008, after steadily rising since 2003, the price of gasoline peaked at over $4.00 per gallon across the United States of America according to AAA. For comparison in January 2003, crude oil prices averaged about $25 dollars per barrel. By July 2008, they topped out at around $147 dollars per barrel. As of early 2012, gas prices continue to hover at over $3.00 per gallon.

The rising oil and fuel prices produced a domino effect like negative impact on businesses across the country. Many businesses that relied on shipping products to consumers were suddenly faced with higher gasoline and diesel prices that adversely affected their bottom line figures. As we all know, when there are negative effects to a company's bottom line there are usually layoffs and position cuts trailing just behind it. Many businesses let go of valuable hard working employees and at the same time passed on the difference in fuel costs to their consumers.

Consumers were hard hit by the high gas prices especially when the time came to fill up their vehicles. In the late 20th century and in the early portion of the 21st, sport utility vehicles were the most coveted new vehicle purchases in the United States. The big three automakers could not build them fast enough to meet the demands of SUV loving consumers. For example, the Jeep Grand Cherokee, at one time the most popular SUV in the country produced by the Chrysler Corporation. The Grand Cherokee has a fuel capacity of about 20.5 gallons. In January of 2003, it would have cost the owner of a Grand Cherokee approximately $32.80 to fill up their vehicle from an empty tank.

By July 2008, filling up the same vehicle would cost an astounding $82.00 dollars. If the owner of the vehicle filled up once a week in January 2003, it would have cost them an average of $131.00 dollars per month. Filling up the same vehicle in July 2008, would have cost them an average of $328.00 dollars per month. The difference over the five-year period with the same vehicle would be almost $200 dollars per month in just gasoline alone. Couple that with the fact that businesses significantly raised their rates on goods and services during that time period. This proved to be a perfect storm leading to financial trouble in the lives of many hard working Americans.

Workers still fortunate enough to maintain employment during the years of outsourcing, bank deregulation and spiking fuel prices faced a myriad of challenges. Many companies enacted freezes on pay raises for their workers who were left behind. In addition to a lack of pay raises, workers were forced to deal with the extra workload left behind in the absence of their laid off or eliminated former co-workers without increased compensation for their efforts. A lot of upper managers then began to flex their muscles by making life more difficult for their remaining employees.

Some examples of this include threatening to fire employees for minor or phantom offenses, and putting their workers in work scenarios expecting them to fail. The morale of workers has dropped all over this country, with workers from all walks of life wondering whether or not there will be a pink slip waiting for them every day they go into work. Millions of people are suffering the effects of stress, insomnia, and anxiety daily.

In light of all that has gone on since 2003, many workers and eliminated workers from all industries have clung to their faiths like never before. They are seeking the comfort of God and are hungry to discover the greater meaning of their lives. People were and have currently been praying to God, "please let me keep my job, or let me find another job." Their prayer should have been, Lord please lead me into the purpose and destiny that you have for my life instead. The truth is you were not created to suffer more than you succeed.

As humans we are creatures of habit and are generally comfortable around individuals with similar life experiences and struggles. For a wide majority of Americans just getting by in life has been good enough for them. They have lived under the impression that living paycheck to paycheck and below it is what normal living consists of. Scores of them have no incentive to improve their situations because doing so would force them to cease operating within their familiar comfort zones. This is compounded by the fact that the majority of their fellow workers and friends hold similar mindsets and live in circumstances similar to theirs.

Laboring Individuals

Inspired by a teaching of Pastor Kevin Adams, I have coined them as laboring individuals. I call them this because they have always labored by doing whatever they have to in order to survive economically. The laboring group of individuals is made up of mostly members of Generation X, Baby Boomers, and their parents. Many of them have spent years working jobs that they absolutely detest. They have done this due to the feeling that they had no other options, or that if their unfulfilling way of life was good enough for their parents, then it must be good enough for them as well. As a result, day after day, month after month, and year after year, they toil in obscurity and frustration while cohabitating with un-kept promise, and unfulfilled dreams. They have either let their dreams spoil, or they try to live their dreams through the lives of their children. They have forgotten that they are never too old to live their dreams. On page 20 I have listed examples of general ideals and concepts common among laboring individuals.

- Exist during the week and live for the weekend
- Work in fields that focus on money while sacrificing meaning
- Feel like they can't reach their destiny because their families and kids are holding them back
- Work hard every day to pay their bills while never getting ahead
- Reluctant to or decline to seek their true purpose
- Believe that dreams are for children and individuals other than themselves
- Listen to what unsuccessful people tell them to do
- Feel their options are limited
- Neglect to live their lives to the fullest
- Hope for the best but always expect the worst in life situations
- See only problems and not the possible solutions to them
- Clueless on how to improve their lives
- Wish for change and improvement in their lives
- Play the lottery and slot machines hoping for a miracle jackpot
- Believe money will solve all of their problems
- Have a limited vision
- Expect only God to make changes in their lives
- Feel that they are insignificant in the grand scheme of life
- Feed their minds and spirits with excuses and reasons why they can't succeed

Functioning Individuals

The next group of individuals is primarily comprised of the children of the laboring individuals, but does include some members of Generation X, Baby Boomers and their parents. A great majority of them grew up watching their parents and grandparents suffer through years of unhappiness and unfulfilled dreams. I refer to this group as functioning individuals.

The functioning individuals are people who want more out of their lives than just paychecks. They have grown up watching the people they love being mistreated on their jobs and downsized as a result of budget cuts. They have made the conscience decision to let the call of God within their hearts lead them as opposed to the call of their bills and bank accounts.

They have understood that the industrial age is over, and have learned to become more self-reliant instead of company dependant. Many of them are now helping the laboring individuals realize that it is never too late to leave the land of security and non-risk for the shores of destiny. In the same manner that I did with the laboring individuals, I have listed the general ideals and concepts of the functioning individuals.

- Make it a point to live every day to the fullest
- Pursue their life calling and have money chase them instead of the other way around
- Feel like they have no choice but to reach their destiny because of their families and inner drive pushing them forward
- Work to honor God by using their gifts and talents
- Go through life doing what they have been called to do
- Choose to discover and live within their purpose.
- Feel their options are limitless

- Unafraid to ask questions about things they do not understand
- Understand that dreams are God's method for shaping their purpose in the pursuit of their destiny
- Steps ordered by God and the desires of their heart
- Live their lives with a sense of urgency
- Hope for the best and expect the best
- Acknowledge problems but accept only possibilities and solutions to them
- Have learned to implement change and strive for self-improvement daily
- Understand that job security is a myth.
- Understand that their jackpot and potential miracles rest inside of them
- Willing to listen for the call of God and abide in obedience to his instructions
- They still thank God no matter if things are going well or poorly for them
- Feed their minds with positivity and their spirits with prayer daily

The Transition from Labor to Function

I implore anyone who reads this and identifies themself as a laboring individual, to please do not let another day go by without attempting to uncover your purpose. There is a stirring within your heart that is leading you to venture outside of your comfort zone. It is God letting you know that he has not forgotten about you, or the gifts and talents he placed within you. The only real difference between laboring individuals and functioning individuals is their perspective.

Believe it or not every single one of us no matter when we were born or our current occupation, or lack there of are functioning individuals. Each of us has a divine calling on our lives to function within our purpose. Those who grew to become laboring individuals allowed fear, doubt, self-defeating thoughts, and other adverse variables to prevent them from either hearing or heeding the call of their names.

They simply have their dials tuned in to the wrong frequency. A lot of them have witnessed functioning individuals listening to the correct frequency and getting blessed with the overwhelming favor of God. Even though they know they are on a frequency that is taking them nowhere, they refuse to change the station. They don't change the station because they have become comfortable living uncomfortably, and it is the only life station they have ever known.

The functioning individuals have seen the toll that years of listening to the wrong frequency has taken on the laboring individuals and have been displeased with what they have witnessed. They understand that the other frequency does exist, but they pay no attention to it due to their focus on fulfilling their divine purpose. They also understand that living within their purpose is the vessel that transports them to the shores of their destiny.

There are however plenty of laboring individuals who have successfully transitioned out of the laboring way of life back into functional living. Their first step in their transition was the renewing of their minds and their willingness to accept change. They had to first believe that the dreams within their hearts were worth fighting for. Once this transition takes place, their frequency changes and the calling within their hearts becomes the only sound they hear.

Chapter 2 Questions

1. Do I feel that my employment is secure?

_____

_____

_____

_____

2. Am I living a comfortably uncomfortable life?

_____

_____

_____

_____

3. Am I laboring in my existence or functioning within my calling?

_____

_____

_____

_____

CHAPTER 3

The Significance Of Listening To The Call

The alarm clock goes off and you are once again battling with yourself to arise from your bed. It becomes harder and harder every day, week, and month after you realize that you are living outside of your purpose and destiny. God has been calling you for a long time but you have successfully dodged him every time. Every day you struggle with the thought of having to get out of bed to make the commute to an unfulfilling workplace. The battle within yourself is far more difficult than the traffic you fight daily going to your place of work. Your work environment brings you no joy, and your paycheck is barely keeping up with the current rate of inflation.

You choose to stay however, reasoning that it is better to have a job that you do not like than to be jobless. Every day you give 100 percent of your best effort on the job and are rewarded with a paycheck, and the opportunity to come back the next day to do it again. Your employer expects you to always give your best effort, and go the extra mile for them daily. The reality has finally hit you that most companies do not care about you or your individual life issues. Their level of care rests in how much production you can give them at the lowest possible rate they can pay you.

The grow up, go to school, and get a good job line has been your personal mantra for as long as you can remember. You may have even gone to college or trade school all in an effort to make your resume look excellent and improve your marketability. You studied hard and piled up massive loans for your sparkling degrees and various certifications. All you have now are debt, frustration, and a lack of career fulfillment.

You have traded in your individuality for a position as a cog in the machine known as corporate dominance. Your life is stuck in the middle of the rat race. An hour of your life is traded in to a company in exchange for a numerical value. For instance, if you make 15 dollars per hour, it represents not just your pay grade, but the amount of money a company feels an hour of your life is worth.

The company controls when you come to work, how much they will pay you, and what tasks they will assign you to work on. For many of you out there this arrangement is what you may have dreamed of. It may be that your calling and gifts are best used in a blue or white-collar job in the middle of the rat race with conditions similar to those listed above. You are the people who go with the flow of your company and are comfortable with your situation. I wish you the best in your pursuit, but please make sure you understand the rules of the game for the 21st century. This chapter will assist you with that task.

For others, there is a level of uncomfort and unfulfillment living this way. There is a hunger for change that burns deep within, but you are unsure how to feed it. You are tired of feeling that you have no control over your existence. In essence both those who hunger for change and those who go with the flow are in the same boat. Unfortunately, both groups are one upper management decision away from being unemployed and looking for work.

If you believe what I say is make believe just take a look at the record number of layoffs and position eliminations between the years 2004-2011 in the United States. The ripple effect has not been confined just to the corporate sector and small businesses, but has trickled down into school districts and government agencies as well. It has not mattered if individuals have been with their companies for 5,10, or 20 years, the rude awakening of pink slips has touched workers in industries once thought of as recession proof. The companies do not care if you have a mortgage, a car payment or a child in college. If eliminating your job is a means for them to trim their budgets and increase profits it has and will continue to be done. It is a harsh way of looking at things, but it is the only real way to do it.

The Need For Transition

Millions of people that are suffering right now are what I refer to as laboring individuals. They have let other people and life's circumstances dictate to them how to live their own lives. They have lived under the bubble of job security and company loyalty for decades. For years they have labored on jobs with no control over the flow of their existence. Many of them are now dealing with the pain of home foreclosures, car repossessions, and the overnight erosion of personal credit scores once built on mountains of consistent payments.

A number of them fortunate enough to find other work have been dealt a rude awakening. A great number of them are now working in jobs where they have little or no experience, at fractions of their previous salaries. I am sure you have seen them; the man at your local grocery store who bags your groceries to perfection, or the lady who looks out of place at your local fast food restaurant who never messes up your order.

Then there are the people who are unable to find work at all. People like Fred the machinist, Joe the plumber, or George the welder. Many of these people went into the workforce directly out of high school or college. They never took the time to listen to the call of God on their life, because at the time the money and growth opportunities were too good to be true for many of them. They did what they had to do to survive, but maybe not what God called them to do.

They have sent out hundreds of resumes and filled out applications all over the country with no success. They have searched for opportunities everywhere but Heaven. God has assigned a Kingdom position with their name on it, which has gone unfilled for many years and several decades in some cases. They have no called and no showed for years, but the grace and mercy of God has still kept them on the payroll of Heaven.

With a lot of the job cuts, layoffs, and general workplace unhappiness, God is telling people that they have ignored his calls long enough. He is waiting for them to call him back because he has an assignment where layoffs or firings don't exist. Each of us has the power to call upon the Lord and never hear a busy signal or an answering machine. He has been patiently waiting for us to seek him out.

It has been a cruel reality for the individuals who have clung to the land of security on the shores of mediocrity and complacency. They have now realized that the land that they thought was secure was nothing more than a fallacy. They assumed they must have been in the right place because there were so many other people in the same position as them. They also felt at home there because the land of security was good enough for their friends and relatives. This helped give them the false impression that there was nothing greater for them to seek in life.

For a lot of people especially laboring individuals, it has taken the near financial collapse of our country for them to entertain the idea of the utter importance of listening to the call of God. They have come to realize they may have to leave the formerly common mindsets they once shared with their friends and relatives behind, and pursue their destiny alone. In order to get the most out of life, everyone must realize at some point, that it is much better to die swimming across the sea of mediocrity and toward their destiny than to exist on the land of false security. This point can only be reached when a person has made up their mind that they are sick and tired of being sick and tired.

These feelings of anger and disgust with their situation cause them to develop a hunger within that is only nourished by the voice of God. This is the place where action and the hunger for application replaces futile talk and frustration. Things that may bring about the need for change are: the loss of a job, watching a friend or relative lose their job, having someone close pass away, realizing that there is more to life than working to pay bills or finally being fed up from the frustration of watching year after year go by without any positive life changes. These are just a few examples of life situations that make people aware of the need for change. Once the need for change is firmly established within the mind of laboring individuals, their transition to functioning individuals begins.

As Americans we have made the mistake of placing too much of our faith in men and money, and too little faith in God and our abilities. So many people have bought into the notion that their companies would take care of them as long as they were productive and worked hard. The days of the loyal employee working for 30 years and then retiring as I stated earlier are long over. That mentality is now a 20th century relic buried in our recent past. The times have changed, and it is time to open up to the concept of self-reliance. Self-reliance is only effective however, when God is ordering your steps and guiding you. There is no other person on this earth who will take better care of you than yourself. Those who cling to the land of security are the people who will someday look back on their lives and wonder what if. Life is far too short and far too precious to live this way. As far as I know, this life is a one shot gift that each and every one of us has the responsibility to maximize.

The Benefits of Living Filled Up

If I get in my personal vehicle and take a 400-mile long road trip, I should theoretically only have to fill up once to reach my destination. If I only filled my tank between empty and ¼ of a tank, I would probably have to make at least 4 or 5 stops in unnecessary places that I have no business being in. Think of your life as if it were a vehicle for a moment. If you are living in the land of security and non-risk, you are doing the equivalent of only filling up your tank less than ¼ of its capacity. If you continue to fill up your tank to the level between empty and ¼ capacity on the road of life, you will frequently be forced to stop in places that you have no business being in.

There are a lot of people out there who feel that living between empty and ¼ of their potential is the only way to get through life. An unwanted by-product of their frequent stops is that they delay or entirely miss out on their destiny due to living at a fraction of their full capacity. Each of us was created to live filled up and topped off to our maximum capacity. There are too many people laboring through life vacillating between empty and a quarter of their designed capacity. They must discover that the journey to them living out God's purpose and destiny will utilize every bit of their fully designated capacity. What will it take to fill you up?

The journey from the land of security to the shores of your destiny will not be an overnight process; it takes months and years to achieve. Take comfort in the fact that the opening of your mind to take the risk to seek your destiny can be made right now as you read this. There is no time to waste, tomorrow is not promised to any of us.

The common refrain from security dwellers also known as laboring individuals is that they will enjoy their lives and maybe follow the dreams of their hearts once they retire. I simply respond to them with the following questions; What if you do not live that long or are incapacitated when that time arrives? What if the stock market collapses when you retire and you lose everything you have worked for?

There is nothing foolproof under the sun. The pursuit of destiny must be mandatory for each of us. There is only one other guarantee on this earth besides death and taxes and here it is. If you choose to listen for and adhere to the call of God in your life, every day will be lived with the renewed fulfillment of your purpose.

I implore you to please not wait until you are older, or let a catastrophic event force you to take action. As of 2012, this world has become more uncertain than at any point in history. Take a chance on living your destiny and making your dreams a reality. Our lives in this world may be uncertain, but take comfort in knowing who holds the world and the certainty of mankind in his hands.

Chapter 3 Questions

1. When was the last time I called Heaven?

_____

_____

_____

_____

2. How much money is one hour of my life worth?

_____

_____

_____

_____

3. What percentage of my full potential am I honestly using daily?

_____

_____

_____

_____

4. Is it better for me to play life safe or take a chance and pursue my destiny?

_____

_____

_____

_____

5. What will it take for me to choose to live my life with a sense of urgency?

_____

_____

_____

_____

CHAPTER 4

God Has Given Us the Tools –
It Is Up To Us To Design The Masterpiece

Placed within each and every one of us are the tools that we need to excel and live life to our designed capacity. There are grams of ability, ounces of excellence, pounds of creativity, and tons of potential in us. A great number of us only take one or maybe two of the tools at a time and actively use them. A small number of us combine them together to live our lives to the fullest design.

Our tools are manifested in different forms. They include our families, co-workers, friends, knowledge learned, lessons gained and even the environments we live in. It is not incumbent on God to design your masterpiece for you. You must take the tools he has blessed you with and apply them to your advantage. For some your tools may place you on the road to being business owners, Doctors, Teachers, CEO's of corporations or even Ministers of the word of God. It all comes down to how you use your gifts and where your greatness reveals itself.

What is the Masterpiece?

We were all specially made by God to fulfill an assignment here on earth. If your assignment was already completed, then your life would already be over. Every day that you live on earth is an opportunity to live within or work toward the completion of your assignment. A great number of people become sidetracked and lose their focus because they spend too much time admiring the masterpieces that others have created. A masterpiece is created when we take our tools and combine them with the gifts that God has placed within us and live as we are called by him to live.

Numerous people are under the impression that they have been sent to earth to suffer, labor, and then die. This is not the case at all. Even though suffering and laboring are a part of life, they are not why we were sent here. We were all sent here to be successful and to live rewarding lives. Not everyone is going to become financially wealthy, but each of us has the capacity to become both financially comfortable and spiritually rich. The latter two elements represent the main theme of the shores of our destiny. However, there are steps that must be taken to get there.

How Is the Masterpiece Created?

We first must recognize that we have been blessed with gifts in the first place. The second step is realizing what our gifts are, and how we can apply them to create personal success. Our gifts are found in the area where our passions lay. When we are passionate about something it allows our gifts to shine through our work. When people see us operating in our gifts, they will know that they are witnessing a combination of God given ability mixed with passion and hard work.

The book of Proverbs chapter 18 verse 16 states, "A man's gift makes room for him, and brings him before great men." My personal definition of success is getting paid financially and/or spiritually to do what you are passionate about while bringing honor to God. God is not going to call you to operate in an area where you will not show passion, or reach your full potential in. He created you and knows what you like and where you can succeed.

There are countless individuals that go through life never acknowledging the possibility of ever living a successful life. They cling to the 20th century mentality of laboring individuals, and have no choice but to live under the terms that life dictates to them. To use a baseball analogy, they would rather get walks and get hit by pitches rather than hit homeruns. If they would just learn to hit the ball (life) hard on the sweet spot of their bats (abilities), they would be giving greatness an opportunity.

When we hit the ball hard on the sweet spot it will reward us with extra bases (a life with purpose) and homeruns (destiny). We were all created with the ability to knock it out of the park, but so few of us do. So many individuals swing with no effort, bunt, or even refuse to step up to the plate at all. If we are not able to use our gifts daily; frustration, anger, disappointment and depression will become our best friends.

Even if you have watched others swing and miss, it should not stop you from pursuing the dreams that God has placed within you. In life when you attempt to live with your gifts dormant you will only manage to exist uncomfortably. It is not okay to live unhappy and uncomfortably within the gift called life. You and I were created to find happiness and enjoy life's journey. I understand there will be times in all of our lives of uncomfort and unhappiness, but they are unworthy of being our long-term companions through this life.

The time has come to turn the tables and dictate to life, how you would like things to be. You possess so much more power than you realize. Your past way of thinking and living must not sabotage your present and future. The fact that you have made mistakes in your past does not disqualify you from being able to discover your purpose and eventually live within your destiny.

How Do I Design My Masterpiece?

When God created you he had an image of what your masterpiece should look like when completed. He knew before you were born what your finished product would become. In the book of Jeremiah chapter 1 verse 5 it states "Before I formed you in the womb I knew you." We were all sent to earth with the necessary tools and a blank canvas to operate from. Our tools and our final masterpiece may be similar to someone else's, but it will not be the same. Are you operating with a blank canvas? If so it is never too late to begin the design process and there is no better time than the present.

The common thread that separates the true artists from the amateurs is hunger. Those that are hungriest are willing to out work or out study anyone to be the best at what they do. For example, each of us is born with the exact same muscles in the same exact location on our bodies. To uncover the muscle and reveal its definition, body fat must be eliminated. This is done when we exercise our bodies. The harder we work on particular parts of our bodies, the more muscle development will be represented there. Repetitions must be done to allow the definition of our muscles to be prominently displayed. Some bodies have more fat than others and others have a higher percentage of muscle. We make the choice how we would like our individual bodies to look.

Our lives are very similar to this example. We were all born with callings of success on our lives. To uncover our best, we must learn how to eliminate the variables that keep us from progressing. How hard we work in the different areas of our lives will show in what we produce. To display the definition of our gifts we must exercise them daily. There is no substitute for putting in the work; it is a step that cannot be skipped.

Each day must be viewed as an opportunity to move closer to your destiny. Are you putting in the work? Are you proud of what you are producing? Your work is only good if you have identified the destination that you are working toward. All of us are good at several different things, but we must pursue what we are great at. Goodness can be rejected, but greatness is truly undeniable. You are great at whatever task you feel allows you to best use your God given gifts and talents to excel in. It is the task that you know in your heart you were created to do.

Please stop standing around watching other people excel in their greatness from the sidelines of life. It is time to get in the game and put your own greatness to the test. You were not created to watch and wish. You were placed here to act and let your life shine as an example of God's infinite power. God gave us each specific tools for a reason. He does not need to explain why he gave us what he gave us. We must figure out what we have and paint like Michelangelo.

Our Choices Are Our Decisions

We are fully responsible for how our lives turn out. No one will follow you around your entire life with a gun trained on you forcing you to make decisions against your will. For a great number of individuals small-minded thinking has yielded small-minded results.

What separated me from many of my peers that I grew up with was my large-minded mentality. What kept me going was the belief that there was a better life outside of the death, and degradation I witnessed every day in my unfriendly neighborhood war zone on the east side of Detroit. As a youngster, I had no concept of purpose or destiny, but I knew that if I followed God, things would get better someday. I learned how to focus and eliminate failure from my circle of friends.

A large number of my youthful peers let their small-minded thinking lead them as adults into small prison cells and small burial plots. They allowed themselves to be swallowed up by our mutual environment. They focused on quick money instead of steady meaning to design their masterpieces with. None of them sold drugs, robbed banks or held up gas stations because it was their passion. It was simply for the money nothing more and nothing less. What is it that guides you?

When you have God, love, and passion leading you happiness is sure to follow. Don't let the pursuit of money cloud your vision in the pursuit of destiny. When you reach your destiny the money will either be waiting for you, or trailing closely behind you. Your life may be in an uncertain place, or you may be living in a rough environment right now. Please do not let small-minded thinking cloud your judgment. You can have a large-minded mentality no matter what stage or life situation you are facing.

The catalyst for a large minded mentality is a strong inner spirit. When your inner spirit is strong you can't go wrong. A lot of people spend so much of their time working on their outer shell that they render their inner spirit weak. A weak inner spirit leaves us vulnerable to suffer from depression, peer pressure, a lack of faith, small-mindedness and cloudy vision.

Our inner spirit is strengthened with positive thoughts, positive actions, positive associations, prayer, knowledge, and most of all a clear vision of our life's purpose and direction. God has given each of us the free will to make choices. Are you happy with the choices you have made? Strive to have a large-minded mentality, and watch your life yield large-minded results and a beautiful masterpiece of God's greatness for the world to admire.

Chapter 4 Questions

1. Why did God send me to Earth?

_____

_____

_____

_____

2. What am I both great at and passionate about?

_____

_____

_____

_____

3. What will it take for me to produce a masterpiece?

_____

_____

_____

_____

4. What size are my thoughts and vision?

_____

_____

_____

_____

Chapter 5

The Casting Call Of Life

The stakes are too high for you not to be successful. Just the fact that you are alive, healthy and cognitive is a blessing itself from God. There are millions of people tethering their lives to the land of false security on the shores of mediocrity. I am sure you know them very well. They want you to stay there with them and it will not be possible. You have a mission to make it to the shores of your destiny and nothing can impede your progress.

These individuals are jaded with life in the box, and wish they could take the risk you are taking by going after your dreams. I call them Spectators; they are first of two subsets of what I referred to as laboring individuals back in chapter two. They are the first of a total of four types of individuals that I will discuss in this chapter.

Laboring Spectators

Spectators in terms of pursuing the dreams of their hearts are fearfully faithless. The only way that they will attempt to make a move is if they know someone who has reached their destiny safely. They have all the ability and gifts from God to make their dreams a reality, but take no action towards making them come true. These people cheer you on and hope for the best for you. They are your friends, family members, and co-workers.

You were once a part of their group until you finally became tired of being sick and tired and decided to use your hunger to facilitate change. For those that you left behind as spectators, you have become their source of inspiration. They pray for you and live vicariously through you. Once they see that you have made it to your destiny, they will have no other option but to try. At least that is what they promise they will do.

The R&B singer Maxwell put it best when he said, "I can let my life pass me by, or I can get down and try to work it all out this lifetime." I could not have said it better myself. These people must understand that they are running their own race, just as you are running your own and that tomorrow is not promised to anyone.

Unfortunately, the spectator group is where a lot of people live their entire lives. They let fears and the paralysis of analysis keep them anchored to the land of false security. They take whatever life throws at them and never find the resolve to fight back. They live content with viewing life from the sidelines. They let the gifts and talents that God gave to them go to waste, because they never muster up the courage to overcome their fears.

God shows them revelations through visions and dreams, but they simply ignore them. The stories about others discovering their purpose and inhabiting the shores of destiny trickle back to them. They are happy for those people, but they never feel like the time is ever right for them to step out on faith in the pursuit of their dreams.

My word to them is, do not be afraid to seek the destiny that God has appointed for your life. Just take a chance, because if you don't try you will miss out on the great things that God has in store for you. Don't go through this life being a person who says I wish I could, strive to be a person who says I already did it. As far as I know this life is a one act show with no sequels in the works. What does it benefit you to live vicariously through someone who has taken action toward fulfilling his or her destiny? The fruition of your destiny is the responsibility of no one other than you.

Laboring Critics

The second group of individuals in our society and a second subset of laboring individuals are Critics. Another common name for them is dream thieves. These individuals are the main cause of spectators relegating themselves to the land of false security. These people promote fear and discouragement to anyone who has dreams of bettering their lives. To reach your destiny they are a hurdle that you must cross. Even Jesus Christ, the greatest man who ever walked the earth, had to face critics. Just like he did, you must overcome the critics to accomplish whatever God has called you to do. Jesus understood that he could not afford for critics to block the plan of God's destiny for him and neither can you.

The critics generally have no business of their own, so they make their existence by meddling in the affairs of others. To escape the land of security and non-risk, the words of the critics must be ignored. They are often miserable people that get their joy in life by making everyone that comes within their vicinity miserable as well. Your failure equals their success. If you are dealing with them, please do everything in your power to filter their negativity out. Doing this protects both your inner spirit and the sanctity of your dreams. There is no way that someone who has gone nowhere in life can help you go somewhere.

Critics are found within your circle of friends, family members, co-workers and even within your place of worship. At times your worst critic can be the person who gazes back at you in the mirror. No matter how much you may succeed in life, the critics will always be there. That is fine as long as you do not allow their criticisms to become rooted within you.

When you allow their criticisms to take root within you, it can rotten out the core of your destiny. The walls of your faith and mental toughness must be fortified to overcome the critics. Whether you believe what God tells you or what the critics say, it is your choice. If you happen to be a critic, it is never too late to change. Learn to be a person who encourages instead of discourages. This simple adjustment in mindset could be the solution that opens your own pathway to the shores of your destiny.

Functioning Actors

The third group of individuals in our society are what I refer to as Functioning Actors. They are the first of two subsets of what I referred to as functioning individuals back in chapter 2.They left the land of false security to pursue the calling that God placed within their hearts. They were able to successfully face their fears and go to the place where God designed and assigned them to be.

They are the people that the spectators cheer for and the critics begrudge. They are the people who transformed their dreams into reality. They did things such as opened up businesses, started ministries, and furthered their educations just to name a few of the myriad of possible examples. These residents of destiny followed God's call to flee the land of false security and reap the rewards of their decision daily.

Every day represents a new chance for them to exercise their passions. They wrote their visions plainly, and executed their plans. They are doing what God created them to do and they know it. These people decided that it was better to move slowly toward their dreams than to stand still hoping to move.

For some actors, their passions will prove to be lucrative financially for them. For all actors their passions will prove to be lucrative in meaning to their lives. According to Mike Illitch, "if you do what you love, the money will come later." Delatorro McNeal says, "Your mint is hidden in your meant." I couldn't agree more with both of them.

Actors are productive within their passions and let the profits pursue them. Their work does not force them to labor but instead challenges them to function within their purpose for living. It did not matter to them what their critics said about them. These people took the criticism directed at them and used it to stoke the fire of their dreams.

There are many of us who will not get the chance to experience life as an actor. This is because some of us do not develop the mental safeguards to deal with the criticisms that will come our way. I will talk more about the importance of mental safeguards in a later chapter. God wants each of us to become actors in the grand production we refer to as life.

There are already enough spectators in Heaven watching over us on earth. We need more actors in this world. When you make the decision to act on the call that God has placed within you, you secure your win for best life picture every year that you live, in the eyes of Heaven. Make it your mission to make our Director proud of his work.

Functioning Actors Emeritus

The fourth group of individuals in our society and the second and final subset of functioning individuals are Actors Emeritus. The actors emeritus are the people that heeded their call from God, lived within it and now devote their lives to helping others heed God's call. They serve as mentors for the actors and sources of encouragement for spectators. They are the treasure givers who impart their wisdom into all those who will listen. They are essentially acting coaches. Their main objective is to continue to live within their purpose daily, and help everyone they can do the same. The actors emeritus not only think outside of the box, they are the blueprints for it. Below I have listed several living individuals who I believe fall into this category.

Robert Kiyosaki
Barbara Walters
Geoffrey Canada
Tony Robbins

Dr. Harry Edwards
Mitch Albom
Joe Weider
Tom Joyner
Les Brown
Jimmy Carter
Oprah Winfrey

The individuals that I have chosen as my actors emeritus come from many different walks of life. The thing that they all share is that they spend a great deal of their time now helping other people reach the shores of their destiny. Their blueprints have helped to inspire scores of younger people ready to take their torches.

These individuals happen to be famous worldwide, but most actors emeritus are not. Most actors emeritus live their lives outside of the white hot gaze of the limelight. There are actors emeritus around you, find out who they are and let them assist you where needed.

Chapter 5 Questions

1. Am I a spectator, critic, actor, or an actor emeritus?

_____

_____

_____

_____

2. What will it take for me to become an actor or an actor emeritus?

_____

_____

_____

_____

3. What do critics say about me?

_____

_____

_____

_____

4. Am I letting the critics prevent me from pursuing my dreams?

_____

_____

_____

_____

PART TWO

Tuesday

BREAKING FREE FROM THE SHACKLES THAT HINDER DESTINY

Chapter 6

Waging The War Versus Fear

In the late 1980's Mike Tyson dominated boxing's heavyweight division with a devastating combination of speed and power. He reigned undefeated for several years laying waste to any challenger that stepped into the ring with him. His greatest asset however wasn't his powerful jab or his devastating right hook; it was his ability to strike fear in his opponents before the opening bell.

When Tyson's opponents stepped into the ring with him and looked into his eyes, they were overcome with the fear of what he may do to them in the fight. Once this happened it rendered the fight over before the toll of the opening bell. Any game plan that Tyson's opponent may have had in hoping to beat him ended when he looked into their eyes. With one look Tyson turned fearless number one contenders into fearful cowards. With one look he would change his opponents mentality from them seeking to win against him to them praying to survive the punishment he would give them. What is your Tyson?

This chapter covering fear and the ones succeeding it will encompass more than just the resources needed to reach your destiny. They will include tools that will help you rise higher in any area of life. Now, let's tackle the first one together.

A major obstacle that prevents many people from living their dreams is the big F. The big F that I am referring to is fear. Fear comes to us in several different forms. Fears that prevent us from seeking our destiny could range from: the fear of failing, the fear of the unknown, the fear of other people's opinions, or even the fear of actually becoming successful in pursuit of your aspirations. I have suffered from each one of the fears above and have finally learned to conquer them. Let me address how to eliminate each one of these fears right now.

The Fear of Failure

The fear of failure is eliminated when you make the decision in your mind that your fear of staying in the same unfulfilling situation becomes less than taking a gamble on your God given abilities. It represents a test of the skill of your ability to choose faith over fear. We overcome it when we make the decision that it is better to go for broke trying, than being broke and/or living an unfulfilled life wishing that we would have, could have or should have tried.

We each are given the option of betting on our gifts and talents in a way that could transform our lives to a level that we are unable to fathom. How can we not take the chance to see what we can do? God loves us too much and he did not create us to fail or to fear failure as well. When you pass away how will you explain to God why you were afraid to step out on faith and use the gifts and talents that he equipped you to excel with. There is no need to put yourself in that situation by wasting the abilities that God has given to you due to the ungodly spirit of fear.

There was a scripture that helped to guide me through this situation when I faced it. In the book of Second Timothy chapter 1 verses 6-8 it says, "Therefore I remind you to stir up the gift of God which is in you through the laying on of my hands. For God has not given us a spirit of fear, but of power and of love and of a sound mind." Some may wonder, what gifts did God give me? We all have several different gifts that we have been blessed with, and we just have to pray and focus, and the answer will await us. To achieve greatness outside of you, you must first believe it lives within you.

Fear of the Unknown

In addressing the fear of the unknown, we have to trust that God is going to lead us through the dark places that we cannot see. That is where our faith plays a critical role in helping us maintain the course to our destiny. Another helper here is education in the particular field in which we would like to be involved in. Education can consist of things like formal study, career shadowing or internships. There is most likely someone living who is doing what it is that you would like to do. Spend some time researching their story, or see if there is someone in your local area who will take you under their wing and show you that the path you seek may not be as unknown as you once thought.

You must ask yourself the question, is it better to be on the path of the unknown or living unknown staring at the path from the sidelines of life? The more education we attain the more confidence we gain. Knowledge truly is power. When it comes to battling any fear especially unknown fears, four of the five types of knowledge that I mentioned in the introduction section will pay huge dividends. I will re-list them just to refresh your memory.

The first type of knowledge is spiritual knowledge. This type of knowledge encourages us to possess a relationship with God, and understand the knowledge of his power and greatness. The second type of knowledge is academic knowledge. It benefits us by providing us with the ability to earn a living and function within the framework of society.

The third type of knowledge we must obtain is life knowledge. It is gleaned through our personal experiences and the life experiences of the individuals we observe and/or admire. It also includes the variable known as common sense. The fourth type of knowledge that we must obtain is field knowledge. This knowledge is gained through learning our desired work fields inside and out. This type of knowledge will help us to become the best workers we can be within our chosen vocation.

When we acquire the four types of knowledge listed above, the unknown will no longer frighten us into being fearful and afraid to proceed with our mission. Our knowledge will equip us with the faith and confidence to meet any challenge that awaits us both within our point of vision or just outside of its scope. The combination of the forms of knowledge listed above will prepare us for success when dealing with any circumstance. In the words of legendary UCLA basketball coach John Wooden, "failing to prepare is preparing to fail." When we are knowledgeable it equals all the preparation we need to succeed.

Fear of Other People's Opinions

When it comes to the fear of people's opinions a good way to avoid this all together is to keep your dreams and desires to yourself. I have a relative that I will not name who has a dream that has been burning in their heart for years and has not acted on it. A big reason for their lack of action is their spouse does not support their dream and feels like it would be a waste of time, money and effort to even pursue the dream.

You must remember that your dreams are your dreams. If God wanted someone else to have the same dreams as yours, he would have placed it in their heart as well. There is no reason that you should allow yourself to be disobedient to God in order to please the needs of someone else. If you know the voice of God is communicating with you through your heart then you must obey his instructions.

Everyone, including those that we love, will not understand the purpose and destiny that God has called us to fulfill. Unfortunately, in many cases, the people who we would hope would be our biggest supporters are our biggest critics. They are often people who mean well, but have never dreamed, or accomplished much in life and would rather criticize and discourage those who are taking action.

It is critical to filter these individuals out and remain focused on your dreams and goals. They are the same people once you are successful who are going to want to take credit for your success and come to you with their hands out stretched. Your dreams represent the roadmap to your destiny, and they must be protected.

Many dreams have been delayed and/or denied due to talented individuals allowing the negative and unconstructive ideas of others to infiltrate the sacred mental real estate reserved for their dreams. It is critical that you only share your ideas and dreams with people who are willing to invest in your dreams with tools such as spiritual, mental, emotional and/or financial support. This is a good way of telling who is genuine about seeing you become successful. You must not let the opinions of others prevent you from fulfilling the assignment that God has placed upon your life. Mediocrity and misery love company, you must not allow them to be guests in your home or tourists in your mind. Entertain greatness and success instead, and I promise things will be better for you.

Fear of Success

The fear of becoming successful is one that many people have faced, myself included. For some of us the thought of actually reaching our destiny can seem a little overwhelming. The solution that allowed me to overcome my fear was by simply thinking about all the lives that I could touch and improve simply using my God given talents to the best of my abilities.

The fact that you are reading this book right now in my mind represents success. Whether I sell one million copies of this book or one hundred, all that matters to me is that someone can take this tool that I have shared and improve their life and that of their community. That is what reaching your destiny is truly about. It is not just about becoming financially comfortable or being able to just enjoy your life every day. It is about being able to enrich the world to the best of your ability by using what God placed within you.

When you die God will not ask you what you purchased or how popular you were on earth. Those things do not matter to him. He is going to want to know who did you help with what he placed within you? How many lives did you touch, and how well did you represent and help build his Kingdom on earth? There is no need to fear being successful. You must take it as a blessing from God that will enable you to then bless his children. He will appreciate it and he will never forget it.

Chapter 6 Questions

1. Which fears are preventing me from pursuing my destiny?

_____

_____

_____

_____

2. What method will best help me overcome my fears?

_____

_____

_____

_____

3. Am I prepared for the destiny that I seek?

_____

_____

_____

_____

4. What method of preparation will best equip me to reach my destiny?

_____

_____

_____

_____

Chapter 7

Respect Is More Valuable Than Gold

Webster's dictionary defines it as a high or special regard. I am referring to respect, which is something that each of us must possess in at least three different forms to reach our destiny. A person must have respect for their individual self, respect for others, and be respected by other people. It is critical to hold a high level of self-respect, or self-esteem as some may refer to it, because it represents the measurement of our personal standards.

Self Respect

I am confident that most of you have heard the Malcolm X quote, "if you stand for nothing you will fall for anything." When you maintain a high level of self-respect, it gives you a solid foundation to stand on. You will refuse to accept substandard treatment, and you will view yourself as a precious commodity. Your level of self-respect is displayed in your everyday words and actions. Without a high level of self-respect, you cheat yourself and the people around you out of your best. You must remember that there is no man or woman in the world who can make you complete. They can only help enhance you or extract from you.

A problem with our current society is that many people have neglected to pay proper respect to themselves. Many of us abuse our bodies with drugs and/or alcohol, or abuse our minds by telling ourselves that we are no good or worthless.

Others allow other individuals to abuse them. The lack of self-respect has led many women to stay trapped in the clutches of abusive situations. It has also caused many men to be abusive verbally and physically so they can feel a level of superiority.

No matter how hard a person may try to hide it, their actions reveal their true level of self-respect. No one who would intentionally hurt another person can truly claim to posses a high level of self-respect for themselves or anyone else. This is due to the fact that when our level of self-respect is high we will not treat another person in a way that we would not want reciprocated. People with low levels of self-respect need others to praise them and need them to feel complete. They have a constant need to be validated. They hide behind Mt. Rushmore's of cars, clothing and jewelry hoping to mask who they truly are from the world.

A common companion of low self-respect is either not knowing who you truly are in this life, or knowing who you really are and not being able to face the reality of it. As people we are similar to onions. We put on a nice glossy shine on the outside with several false layers to protect our roots behind it. Our roots are where our inner spirit resides within our hearts.

What kind of onion are you? Are you a fresh onion with fresh layers hidden behind your glossy outer peel? Your sweet aroma projects a high level of self-respect. Or are you a spoiled onion with rotting layers hidden behind your glossy outer peel? It really doesn't matter what your glossy outer peel looks like, or what you say you are. The scent you project will reveal your identity in due time.

Before we can know who we are and find comfort in it, we must know whose we are. We are children of God and deserve to be thought of and treated that way. Many of us put up false layers to project an image of ourselves in an attempt to impress people. When we do this, we run the risk of living a lie for so long that we forget what our true self originally resembled. Even though it may be difficult, learning to love and respect ourselves is paramount in reaching our destiny.

A high level of self-respect is critical both in our personal lives and in business. Our level of self-respect gives people a clear illustration of where our boundaries lay, and how far they may advance in relation to them. The only thing worse than mistreating someone, is allowing yourself to be mistreated. Every day all over the world people allow themselves to be treated any kind of way to protect their careers and/or relationships. Are they really worth it? Are you not a child of God?

If we lead our households, and expect our children to carry themselves with a high level of self-respect, what is preventing us from following our own message? The time for being a hypocrite has passed, and its time that we practice what we preach. When a person possesses a high level of self-respect, it will keep them strong and safely on the pathway to their destiny. Self-respect will keep you standing for something when others around you are falling for any and everything.

Respect For Others

An excellent representative of our character is the manner in which we treat other people. The general rule of thumb is to treat others how we would like to be treated; there are multitudes of us that have fallen short in this area. Simply because many people do not acknowledge it, does not mean it is okay for us to disregard it. Jesus Christ gives us these words in the book of Luke chapter 6 verse 31, "And just as you want men to do to you, you also do to them likewise." This is not just an Eric Moore principle but also a heavenly inspired principle. The reason this principle is important, is that it helps foster an environment filled with peace and harmony within our lives. The energy we project into the world will be the energy that is returned. Scores of senseless crimes have been committed due to individuals feeling disrespected.

Respecting someone does not mean kissing up to them, groveling in their presence or agreeing with their every word. We do not threaten, coerce or abuse in any way the people that we respect. True respect is first acknowledging that we are all brothers and sisters in the eyes of God. When we respect others we make them aware of their value to us. When we respect others we neither fear them nor intimidate them. We do not place them on a pedestal or look down upon them. We see them as equals living their lives parallel to ours.

Respect for others opens up our ability to empathize and allows us to acquire the perspective from which others visualize the world. To get respect we must give it, and to give our respect we must see it given to us. The fact that we respect a person does not mean that we may always respect the decisions that they make. It is entirely possible to respect a person and not their actions. If there is a lack of respect then peace and harmony will not prevail. Many of the ills of our society could be solved if people would just learn to have respect for one another.

There is no person on this earth who is greater than any of us. In the same token, we are no greater than anyone else on this earth either. What separates us is the great or poor decisions that we make in relation to the circumstances that life places before us. All men and women are created equally in the eyes of God. When other people respect us and they know that we respect them, it makes them want to work hard with us and for us. We command it as a result of our actions and give it via our words and the actions that support them.

If we were customers at a business and felt that we did not receive good customer service, how would it shape our impression of that business? Would we choose to do business with that company again? Would we recommend or have a positive opinion of that company to give to others? Most all of us would answer all three of those questions with a resounding no.

Our lives are very similar to this concept. When we display our respect for other people it is essentially our personal form of customer service. Other people use our level of respect for others as a barometer of our character. If we develop a consistent pattern of treating people with respect, it will give our names and reputations a priceless value.

Respect From Others

Being respected by others will entice anyone coming your way to behave properly in your presence. When people respect you they are more likely to listen to you and hold you in high regard. Respect from other people is earned only through your actions. It cannot be purchased, negotiated or commandeered through coercion. Those of us who prove ourselves trustworthy and live by our words are generally universally respected.

As a young boy I would often ask my grandfather, what is the measure of a man? Every time I asked him his response was always the same. In his eyes what made a true man was someone who backed up their words with the actions that matched them. It was someone who made their words their bond and took care of all of their responsibilities. For some who may read this, it may be old school philosophy, but in my eyes it is the only way to live. In today's society if more of us lived by that philosophy there would be less lying to ourselves and to other people.

When we develop a reputation for enforcing our word and handling business properly it makes people gravitate to us. To be respected by others, we must possess both a high level of self-respect and respect for others. No one is going to respect us if we choose not to respect them or ourselves.

When you reach your destiny there will be no need to talk about how great you are. If you are truly respected and appreciated, others will do the talking for you. Your occupation, financial predicament, family name or good looks do not earn the respect of others. It is built on a foundation of honesty, integrity, fairness and consistency earned over time. What are the elements of your foundation of respect?

Chapter 7 Questions

1. Do I have respect for myself?

_____

_____

_____

_____

2. Do I consistently show respect for other people?

_____

_____

_____

_____

3. Am I respected by other people?

_____

_____

_____

_____

Chapter 8

Overcoming Unforgiveness

Numerous individuals are living with their eyes trained on their past instead of on their prize. We must all learn to get over our past before we can enjoy true happiness when we reach our destiny. As believers in God, we must learn to achieve forgiveness in at least three critical forms.

We must learn to forgive ourselves, forgive others and seek God's forgiveness. Many times in our lives we will have flashback moments to past situations and realize that we should have made different decisions. We gaze back through the cinema of our mind with regret. We then feel the need to punish ourselves because the person who wronged us stares back at us in the mirror daily.

Forgiveness of Self

The lack of forgiveness within causes turmoil and disrupts the flow of our inner spirit. It is the equivalent of trying to drive a vehicle with the transmission stuck in neutral and the hazard lights flashing. We look around and see other cars (people) moving past us and it makes us angry. We wonder why no one will stop and show pity on us or ask us if we are doing okay. They do this simply because all they see is the anger in our faces and not the pain in our hearts. Our expression serves as a deterrent to anyone that comes in contact with us.

We sit with our lives in neutral staring at the skyline of God's destination for us far off in the distance. We give ourselves the false impression that whatever we did wrong convicts and sentences us to a mandatory life sentence of misery. Good Samaritans who may attempt to help us unknowingly walk into our Bermuda Triangles of anger, despair and depression.

My friends this is no way to live. It is not how God wants us to live either. There is no rewind or pause button for your life. Once a moment passes it is gone forever. It really does not matter what you may have done, God does not keep score of your past sins and neither should you. In the book of Micah chapter 7 verse 19 it states, "He will again have compassion on us, and will subdue our iniquities. Thou will cast all our sins into the depths of the sea."

If the Lord will give you a clean slate for your past mistakes, why don't you start forgiving yourself today? Your past mistakes and failures are your greatest teachers in life. You must learn to help others to not make the same mistakes you made and shift your life back into drive mode. Just because you were stuck in neutral for a while does not mean that your destiny has vanished. Once you decide to forgive yourself, you will once again move forward and become much closer to your destiny than you could have ever imagined. You are your own best friend on this earth, and a friendship without love and forgiveness is no friendship at all.

The Forgiveness of Others

For a great number of people forgiveness of themselves is not hindering their progress, it is the lack of forgiveness of others that they withhold. People can undoubtedly hurt you with their words and/or their actions. A person can only put you through as much personal hell as you allow them to. More often than not the person you hold unforgiveness toward has long moved on with their life and are not thinking about what they did to hurt you. Some of us struggle with the fact that they have moved on and it upsets us that they have not suffered. We desire revenge against them to make them feel just a fraction of the hurt that has engulfed us. In the Apostle Paul's letter to the Romans chapter 12 verse 19 this is addressed. Paul writes, "Beloved, do not avenge yourselves, but rather give place to wrath; for it is written, Vengeance Is Mine, I will repay, says the Lord." With that verse God tells us not to worry about our wrongs being avenged, that he will take care of the situation.

If you go through life unable to forgive others it can cause you serious complications within your life. People that harbor unforgiveness tend to have physical illness afflicting their bodies and blocked blessings due to clogged spiritual arteries. It is crucial as humans that we learn to let go, and let God fight our battle. When we learn to let go we free our spirit to flow freely. When we let go we are able to learn to give people a chance and not punish those around us for what others may have done to us.

The longer we hold on to unforgiveness, the longer the hurt and pain will linger. It does not matter if someone abandoned us, or if someone physically or verbally scarred us. We must know that God is and has always been in control. We must seek comfort and peace from him and know that he loves us no matter what may have happened in our past.

For a great number of people forgiving someone who has wronged them may be the most difficult pill they may have to swallow. It is not an overnight process, but they can someday reach it with God's unchanging hand as their guide. Allow no one to steal the joy that is inside of you. You must not let unforgiveness block your blessings and prevent you from becoming all that God has called you to be. Many people claim to have forgiven someone, but they rehash it and hold the issue over their head. This is convenient forgiveness, but not true forgiveness. When you truly forgive you must give up any feelings of resentment and the desire for the other person to be punished by you.

You can forgive others, but it is imperative that you not forget what happened. When you choose not to forget, it equips you with the ability to help others going through what you went through. It also permanently places you on guard to protect yourself from ever being wronged again in the same manner. Your ability to not forget serves as your battle scar and proof of how God delivered you through the war of unforgiveness and pain.

The Forgiveness of God

When we have done wrong to ourselves, or others, we need to seek God's forgiveness. None of us here living on this earth is perfect. We all make mistakes. It is a greater mistake however to dwell on those mistakes and not advance in your journey. Human nature convinces you to throw pity parties, while God is looking to oversee your victory celebrations. There is no sin under the sun that God cannot deliver you from. When you ask him for forgiveness you must be sincere.

Your level of sincerity is not measured in how many tears you shed, or how many times you ask for his forgiveness. The sincerity is displayed in how you choose to live after you request God's forgiveness. Empty words must be transformed into heavy actions that demonstrate contrition. When we continue to make the same mistakes over and over again, it shows him that we are not growing nor are taking our plea of contrition seriously. It also undermines the gift of forgiveness that we asked him to grant us in the first place. Crying wolf is not allowed when we go to God. We must go to him earnestly seeking to improve our behavior.

What about murderers, rapists, drug dealers and other people that have lived lives promoting evil? He forgives them all. The blood that Jesus shed on the cross on Calvary cleanses all of our sins away. It may not seem right to us, but he forgives all those who ask for his forgiveness and are sincere.

When he was on the cross awaiting his crucifixion at the hands of the Roman government, he was asked to be forgiven by a thief being crucified next to him. In the book of Luke chapter 23 verse 43 Jesus states, "Assuredly, I say to you, today you will be with me in paradise." This verse illustrates that no matter what you may have done, God still cares about you and his hand is always outstretched waiting to forgive you. Even though we may feel that certain other people or our individual self should not be forgiven, it is not our decision.

God makes the decision on whether to forgive us or not. He is the only one with the power to place us in Heaven or Hell. The fact that you may have done wrong in your life does not exclude you from the blessings and love of the creator. We all may fall off the path to our destiny, but the true crime is staying off the path.

You must humble yourself by sincerely asking God for forgiveness and get back on the pathway towards your destiny. Unforgiveness has delayed or denied destiny for countless individuals. The time has come for you to grab on to God's unchanging hand and let him lead you through unforgiveness and toward your destiny.

Chapter 8 Questions

1. Is my unforgiveness of myself or others keeping my destiny delayed or denied?

_____

_____

_____

_____

2. Is my lack of unforgiveness worth the sacrifice of my destiny?

_____

_____

_____

_____

3. Do I understand that God will forgive me for anything I have done as long as I ask him sincerely?

_____

_____

_____

_____

Chapter 9

All Eyes On You

In his 1984 hit R&B singer Rockwell lamented the fact that he always felt like someone was watching him. He was correct in his assessment. Someone truly was watching him, it was God. As of 2012, there were more than 6 billion people accounted for all over the world. Every one of these individuals has the eyes of God trained squarely on them. They also have the eyes of their families, friends and associates placed on them as well. It does not matter where you lay your head at night, or inhabit during the day, there will be eyes on you. All of our struggles, cries, successes and triumphs are all being watched.

Each one of our lives is a reality show. Are you G rated, PG, PG 13, R or NC 17? What is your life reflecting? Would your life be dramatic, comedic, action packed or psychologically thrilling if it were being recorded? How much better would we live our lives if we acknowledged that we were constantly being watched? Would we be more truthful, stop cutting corners and try daily to give the best performance we can give.

The Importance of High Character

There are many people who desire to reach their destiny, but are prevented by not performing to the best of their abilities right where they are. How can we be trusted with large increase and promotion if we do not handle business where we are? Many of us lie, cheat and steal trying to get ahead. Those of us who do those things justify it by saying that we have seen other people do those things and seemingly get blessed right before our eyes.

The truth is it really does not matter what others do to seemingly get ahead. That is why we run our own race within this life. What God has planned for you is for you only. He could simply be testing your level of obedience to see if you are worthy of being elevated. Having excellent character and doing things the right way will take and keep you far ahead of those who do not.

When you cut corners in life, you will burn out and your success will not last. Having excellent character means that you do what is right when you feel that no one is watching you. It may seem that people are accomplishing their goals without it, but their success will be fleeting. Even though it may seem at first like you will not get ahead, you must continue to concentrate on your race. When you do this, you will surpass the unjust eventually. Lies and cheating may get them in the door, but excellent character will help you own the building.

Being a person of excellent character will garner you respect from the pulpit to the prison yard and all places in between. What is done in the dark will eventually be revealed in the light. Are you proud of what you do in the dark? When we prove to God that we can display excellent character at all times, he will promote and ease the pathway to our destiny. Do not be afraid of doing what is hard when others take the easy route by cutting corners. The easy way isn't always the best way.

A great number of people have allowed a lack of excellent character to drown their potential destiny within the sea of mediocrity. Without excellent character greatness cannot sustain itself. It is excellence that serves as the umbilical cord of greatness. We must strive to live a life that we would be proud to display if we knew that someone was watching us at all times. In the words of Abraham Lincoln, "Character is like a tree and reputation like its shadow. The shadow is what we think of it; the tree is the real thing." We are the only ones in control of our character. In this world our names precede our arrival and character is our catalyst.

God is not the only one who watches you. There are people all around you watching you as well. Each of us is one person away from a life-changing blessing. It is important that we stay on our toes, 24 hours a day, 7 days a week, and 365 days a year to put it figuratively. As I said earlier, God is not going to simply drop a life raft upon us. We must prove that we are swimming toward our destiny.

The level of character that we display in the dark or in the light, prove whether we are swimming on the right path toward our destiny. Below I have listed examples of several individuals who exemplified excellent character in the 20th and early 21st centuries. This group of names was chosen because of the respect that they each have garnered in their respective disciplines. Respect is the fruit of all character.

Dr. Martin Luther King	Social Activist
Mahatma Gandhi	Social Activist
John Wooden	Retired NCAA Coach
Tony Dungy	Retired NFL Coach
Avery Johnson	NBA Coach
Oprah Winfrey	Entertainment Mogul
Billy Graham	Evangelist
TD Jakes	Evangelist
Barack Obama	44th US President
Mother Teresa	Missionary
Jackie Robinson	Baseball Pioneer
Jon Huntsman Jr.	Politician
Dolly Parton	Country Singer
Lee Haney	Bodybuilder

Integrity

The running mate of character is integrity. It is a combination of honesty and sincerity. Our level of integrity illustrates the codes by which we live to others. It is important that you are known as a person who is trustworthy and can be counted upon. There is a premium on individuals who are genuine and can be trusted.

When you live a life with integrity, your name and reputation are golden. People will look up to you as someone they would aspire to be like. When an individual possesses both a high level of character and a high level integrity, their presence illuminates any room they walk in. It is a feeling as if greatness enters the room every time they appear.

When you walk into a room, people should be able to see you and feel positive energy. It is your duty to set solid examples for people who look up to you especially children. Wherever you go on this earth, you represent several different groups of people. Take a look below at a few of the groups that I represent with my life.

Christians	African Americans
People under 35	My Family
Writers/Speakers	College Graduates

The examples listed above are just a few groups that I represent. What groups do you represent? Take the time to fill in the box below just as I have on the above.

Whenever we walk into a room we represent the many different groups that we listed above. Whenever we meet people we may be the only representative of our groups that they have ever met or tried to get to know. We must proudly represent our groups and do them all justice with our words and actions. Who knows, the person we just met could represent the revelation of the life raft to destiny that we have been searching for.

Without a high level of character and/or integrity we could miss out on the blessing that God may be attempting to grant us through others. High character and integrity equip us with the strength to stay afloat on our path to destiny. We must each strive to be people who bring out the best in others. When someone comes in contact with us they should be proud to know or have met us. Once we do this, our pathway to destiny will become much easier.

Room For Humor

A great character trait is the ability to have a sense of humor. It is no fun to go through life without having fun. No one wants to be around someone who is grumpy and miserable every day. If some of us would smile a little more, it would help us to realize that the gift of life isn't so bad. Having a humorous side can do positive things for both our state of mind and stress level. Whenever we smile it opens a window to our soul allowing others a peak inside.

A person that lives their life with excellent character, integrity and a sense of humor can persevere through any situation that life throws their way. You should look to surround yourself with people that won't lie to you, are genuine and make you laugh. McDonalds would be hard pressed to create a better combo than that. Always remember that someone is watching you, please put on a show that you would be proud to display.

Chapter 9 Questions

1. Am I a high character individual?

_____

_____

_____

_____

2. Is a lack of high character keeping my destiny delayed or denied?

_____

_____

_____

_____

3. Am I a person of integrity?

_____

_____

_____

_____

4. Is a lack of integrity causing my destiny to be delayed or denied?

_____

_____

_____

_____

5. If my levels of character and/or integrity are in question, what steps can I take to improve them?

_____

_____

_____

_____

Chapter 10

Claiming The Victory Over Stress

Quite simply stress will kill you. Everyone no matter who they are will face stress at some point in life. It is not a matter of if, but when we will face it. Whenever we face it, we must all learn to deal with and manage it properly. Our destinies and lives depend on it. Stress and its various by-products have caused many people to miss their appointment with destiny.

With stress comes depression, anxiety, illness and even premature death. Our ages, gender, ethnicity and religious affirmations have no way to insulate us from stress. If anyone reading this has never dealt with stress, my advice is to just keep on living it will come at some point. The root of so many of our problems is stress. Below in random order I have listed several causes of stress in our lives.

Having more bills than the money to pay them
The present and future condition of our world
The death of a loved one
A job loss or income reduction
Health difficulties personal, family or friends
Relationship difficulties
Unhappiness with how our life has gone or its direction
Workplace difficulties

Depression
Feeling guilty about something we have done in our past
Holding on to unforgiveness and bitterness
Feeling trapped in negative situations
Overall career unsatisfaction
Feeling that God has abandoned us or is upset with us for our past mistakes
Feeling that we have abandoned our relationship with God and are unable to reconnect

Below I have listed several solutions for stress in random order.

Finding proper life balance keeping (1st God 2nd Family and Friends 3rd Occupation)
Seeking out our true life purpose
Physical Exercise
Talking about our issues with someone we can trust such as: a close family member or friend, therapist, support group etc
Taking a mental break from our issues if possible
Talking about our issues with God through prayer
Looking for and acknowledging any positive aspect of our issues
Participating in a hobby that we love
Listening to inspirational or relaxing music such as gospel or jazz
Reading positive inspirational books or other written material such as this one
Searching the Bible for a situation similar to ours

Finding something to laugh about such as a funny movie or television program
Learning to forgive ourselves and others
Doing something positive for someone else
Believing that God has the final word concerning any matter

The top 3 causes of death in the United States of America are Heart Disease, Cancer and Stroke, according to the Centers for Disease Control. Many of the people that have lost their lives to these conditions lived stressful lives. We must learn to control stress and not let it control us. There is no way that we can truly reach the destiny that God has for us if we go through our lives stressed out.

Stress clouds our vision and prevents us from examining the big picture of our lives. Stress blinds us to the possibilities of our potentially positive futures. Learning to effectively manage stress is a skill that all destiny seekers must learn to master. The stressful circumstances of life has caused too many individuals to abandon the promise of their destiny that God has placed in their hearts.

In the book of Matthew chapter 6 verses 25-27, Jesus offers us insight as to why we should not worry. He states, "Therefore I say to you, do not worry about your life, what you will eat or what you will drink; nor about your body, what you will put on. Is not life more than food and the body more than clothing. Look at the birds of the air, for they neither sow nor reap nor gather into barns; yet your heavenly Father feeds them. Are you not of more value than they? Which of you by worrying can add on a cubit to his stature?" In the same way that God provides for birds, he provides for us humans as well. God does not want us to worry about solutions that only he can provide.

Taking Care of Ourselves

If you happen to ride on an elevator, you will notice that inscribed on its wall is a weight capacity. When more and more people get on the elevator, it will not function as it did with just one person on it. The closer that the weight it carries gets to its capacity, the elevator will send a warning signal that the poundage on it is getting too close to its weight limit. The elevator will begin to make unusual noises to signal its stress. This is a warning sign that we are treading too close to the maximum amount of weight it can handle.

If the weight capacity of the elevator is exceeded, it will cause the elevator to cease working properly and render it out of order. The elevator can only take so much stress before it will break. In the worst of circumstances, the cable in the elevator shaft could snap, which could result in serious injury or death to its occupants. In another instance the elevator could get stuck leaving its occupants with no other recourse but to call for emergency help. Once the help arrives and the occupants are rescued, the elevator manufacturer must go in and repair the damage done to it.

Our minds and bodies are just like elevators. Each and every one of us has a breaking point. Our minds and bodies can only handle so much stress before we have a breakdown. We pile so much junk into our minds that we neglect to filter it out. The stress on our minds becomes so heavy that it manifests itself into negatively affecting our bodies. Our body then begins to attack itself. We have warning signs such as: high blood pressure, high cholesterol, chronic illness, the inability to focus, weight fluctuations, and mental and physical fatigue just to name a few. Our bodies try to warn us that we are edging dangerously closer to our breaking points.

What ultimately will happen is that we will stress ourselves directly into the cold clutches of illness or death. Many of us will have fatal heart attacks or strokes as a direct result of the stress that we allow to arrest our minds and imprison our inner spirits with negative thoughts. Those that survive heart attacks or strokes are left with irreparable damage to both mind and body. Others may not have heart attacks or strokes, but are left stranded within the stranglehold of chronic illness with peace of mind nowhere to be found. These individuals who survive are left with no choice but to call on the creator in Heaven to help them back to safety. They then realize how fortunate they are that stress did not kill them or cause damage that could not be treated.

There is someone reading this currently that has been broken down by stress. You have come to the realization that it was nothing but God's grace and mercy that pulled you through it. There is also someone who may be close to their breaking point and may not know what to do. Please recognize that there is no situation too large for our God to handle. Whatever the situation is that troubles you, remember that there is a solution for the situation. His name is Jesus Christ. Take the time to let him know what has you stressed out and trust that he will take care of it. For some of us finding someone that we trust may be the solution that God wants for us. For others it could be exercising or finding something that will make us laugh. These simple solutions are just a few examples of remedies that filter out the effects of stress.

Controlling Stress

Stress is only able to affect us as much as we allow it to. There is no need to wait until you have a heart attack or stroke before you make it a priority to control your stress level. It is impossible to make it to the shores of destiny deceased, in a hospital bed, or strapped in a straight jacket. If Presidents Clinton, Bush and Obama all found time in their day to exercise, we can find time for our own stress solutions as well. Stress left unfiltered is similar to a house fire left uncontrolled. It must be contained and properly handled before it spirals out of control. If it is not controlled, the flames of stress will engulf our lives. God has provided us with several different options to extinguish the flames of stress, but it is up to us to properly utilize them.

There are so many of us that constantly stress over issues that are out of our control. We may not be able to control the issues, but we do have the power to control how we react to them. The word tells us that God will never allow more strain on us than we can bear. He designed us with individual capacities to handle stress. Some people are able to handle more stress than others due to their larger capacity. No one is stress proof however. What may be a stress solution for one person may not work for someone else. Each one of us must figure out our personal stress filtration mechanism and apply it when necessary. Stress is a dream thief and a predator of destiny fulfillment.

When we allow stress to control us, we grant it more power over our lives than God. Stress makes our minds focus on it instead of God, or the options we have to keep it in check. Simply taking a step back from our situation and clearing our minds can make a world of difference. Another benefit when we take a break from our situations is it allows us the opportunities to find positive aspects within our situations.

Taking a step back allows us the chance to step up and control the situations that are stressing us. When we learn to slow things down and look at them objectively, we tend to make better and informed decisions on our own behalf. Being prideful and maintaining the idea that we are bullet proof will lead to stress winning the battle against us. It is critical that we swallow our pride and learn to seek assistance when we need it.

If your stress is financially related, there is no shame in seeking assistance from someone who is knowledgeable in that area. If it is health related, you must not be afraid to visit a physician or other medical professional for assistance. Even if you lack health insurance there are organizations in place to help you get the help that you need. If your issue that stresses you is spiritual, there are qualified clergymen and women ready to assist you. If your problem is within your family or other relationships there are counselors, psychologists and other individuals qualified to help you get through. In the same manner that you attack your fears of the unknown, you must attack stress as well. You must use the power of knowledge to aid you in your battle against stress.

Over and above all these things God and Jesus Christ can help you make it through any situation that I listed and any others not listed. There must be success over stress for you to reach your destiny. You must be determined not to let stress win its battle against you. God has placed the proper people in the correct positions on earth to help us get through the stressful circumstances of life. There are many people that have the attitude that they can either figure things out themselves or that God alone will fight their battles. They fail to realize that those solutions alone will not work for everyone or for every situation.

We must understand that God in the same manner that he equipped us for life has also equipped others to help us as well. It may be God's will for us to seek the help of a qualified professional in whatever area that stresses us. We must ask God for vision and favor, so that we can be where he needs us to be to receive the assistance we need. When God sees that we are proactive in helping ourselves, he will send every resource possible to aid our efforts.

Winning on Offense

This reminds me of the story of the homeowner who was told about the flood coming his way. He knew in is heart that God was going to save him and take care of him during the flood. Before the floodwaters began to rise a neighbor asked if he would like to ride with him to escape the ensuing flood. The homeowner replied no thank you; God will take care of me. The floodwaters began to rise and someone in a boat offered him a chance to ride away to safety. The homeowner politely refused and stated that God would take care of him.

The floodwaters then rose so high that it forced the homeowner to flee into his attic to escape the floodwaters. Finally, a rescue helicopter then flew by and offered him a chance to fly away to safety. He refused and replied that God would save him. Ultimately, the man drowned in the flood. When he got to Heaven he asked God, why didn't you save me? God replied I tried to save you. I sent a car, a boat, and a helicopter.

Many times God looks to bless us through the people that he places in our path. We must all keep an open mind and understand that God may be calling on us to call upon someone he has placed in position to help us. All we must do is ask God to compel the anointing of his Holy Spirit to guide us.

The power of God's Holy Spirit must be activated and alive within us. We are much too blessed to go through life held captive by stress. A heavy burden is lifted off our shoulders when we finally learn to control stress. When this is done it allows the voyage to our destiny to become much easier to navigate. Stress reduction is a lifestyle adjustment. None of us are machines, we are human beings created in the image of God.

There are so many people who try to hold so many things inside, because they feel it is the only way to show their strength. They hold on to anger, grief, unhappiness, unforgiveness and bitterness. As a remedy for their situation they attempt to cover up the problems that plague their inner spirits. Many of them become victims of various addictions, alcoholics and even workaholics. These are common symptoms of people trying to cope with painfully stressful situations. These individuals just want something to take their minds off the pain they have been dealing with.

They are essentially using a temporary solution to remedy a permanent problem. The stress builds up within them and eventually manifests itself in the form of poor decisions and irrational behaviors. It is true that everyone deals with stressful situations differently, but the key is to deal with them head on. I understand this will be difficult and painful, but it is utterly essential in our quest to move forward in life.

The Benefits of Victory

We all must learn to take personal time for ourselves to heal our minds and spirits. When we do this, it allows us to face down the issues that stress us at our full strength. It is imperative that we truthfully examine our situations for what they are and not what we would like them to be. It is not a sign of weakness to admit that we need a break or another form of assistance with whatever stresses us.

It is both a sign of courage under fire and strength under duress. It is up to us to turn the problems that stress us into possibilities that benefit us. There is no one on earth who has the ability to take better care of us than we can. It is inherent upon us to acknowledge when we need time to ourselves and take it.

The individuals that truly succeed in this life take the issues that stress them and transform them into the fuel that powers their dreams. They learn to turn the tables on stress by using it as a motivating force instead of an entity that will defeat them. They develop a battle plan to attack stress before it attacks them. To reach our destiny, we must go on the offensive and be proactive in attacking the issues that stress us. It may not be an easy task for many of us, but it must be done. Our lives and destinies depend on it.

Dr. Martin Luther King

Take a look at the life of Dr. Martin Luther King as an example of what attacking the issues that cause stress can do for our self and for others as well. Dr. King could have easily made up his mind that this country would never change and that he and his successors would be resigned to live their lives under the weight of Jim Crow segregation. He understood that there was work needed to be done to fight the negative issues that plagued the southern United States, in the early to mid 20th century. Dr. King made up his mind to roll up his sleeves and do whatever work was necessary to strike back at the racial inequality that plagued our country.

With God's assistance and inspired by the work of Mahatma Gandhi, Dr. King and his associates developed a battle plan featuring non-violent resistance as their chief objective. Their plan proved to be effective in combating the proponents and components of Jim Crow separate but unequal laws. He personally helped get civil rights legislation passed and began a process that has provided for us a country to live in free from legislated Jim Crow laws and legal segregation. The impact of Dr. King attacking the issues that stressed him, has resulted in a much better country for those of us who have inhabited it in the years following his movement.

Your attack plan against the issues that stress you may not affect the country like Dr. King was able to. It will however affect your life and the lives of those who come in contact with you. Imagine if Dr. King would have never taken the offensive approach to the issues that stressed him.

Thank God we will never have to know, simply because he decided that his life was too blessed to be engulfed by the stresses of racism. Your battle may not be with Jim Crow laws or segregation, but a personal battle plan must be developed for you nonetheless. You must be willing to help yourself in order to defeat stress. Your power to conquer stress is contained within the solutions that you decide work best in your fight against it.

Your first step is acknowledging that you are in a battle with stress and that your job is to develop an attack plan and implement it. God will be there guiding you through the battle but he is counting on you to do your part. When God is leading you he will provide a pathway for your success. Failure is and never has been his claim to fame. The same God that helped Dr. King triumph over injustice is the same

God who will help you win the battle over stress and lead you to the shores of your destiny.

In the book of John chapter 14 verses 26-27 Jesus states, " But the comforter, which is the Holy Ghost, whom the father will send in my name, he shall teach you all things, and bring all things to your remembrance, whatsoever I have said unto you. Peace I leave with you, my peace I give unto you: not as the world giveth, give I unto you. Let not your heart be troubled, neither let it be afraid." God has sent his Holy Spirit to assist us in the battle against stress and offer us peace that surpasses all understanding. The peace that we will receive will come from the hand of God. With the aid of the Holy Spirit, soon we will win all battles in our war against stress.

Chapter 10 Questions

1. Is stress delaying or denying my destiny?

_____
_____
_____
_____

2. What methods do I use to help me control my stress level?

_____
_____
_____
_____

3. Do I use temporary solutions to solve long-term issues?

_____
_____
_____
_____

4. Have I gone to God in prayer concerning the issues that stress?

_____

_____

_____

_____

5. What is my attack plan to conquer stress with?

_____

_____

_____

_____

Chapter 11

Focusing On Money Instead Of Purpose Leads To Heartache And Headache

Just as Heaven is the reward for living a life pleasing to God, money is the earthly reward for solving a specific societal problem. A large problem in our society is that we have become so money hungry in this world, that we have lost our appetite for God. The acute lack of money has caused for some of us the fabric of our morality to wane. In the same token, a lack of defined life purpose causes our destiny to be denied. In his first letter to Timothy chapter 6 verse 10, the Apostle Paul stated, "For the love of money is a root of all kinds of evil, for which some have strayed from the faith in their greediness, and pierced themselves through with many sorrows."

Neither he nor I are against individuals becoming financially wealthy or comfortable in this world. Money is a great tool that has the ability to open both windows and doors of blessings for God's children. It also is a tool that has the power to create a lifestyle of freedom, which can grant us more control over our daily existence.

The pursuit of it becomes an issue when our quest for financial advancement prevents us from doing what God has commanded of us. The single-minded pursuit of money has caused many of us to miss out on the calling that God has placed within our hearts. Each of us must determine exactly what guides our motives. It is an individual assignment that only we can figure out.

What is Leading You?

There are many of us who have been led by the compass of money instead of the compass of our hearts. When we lead with our pocketbooks it tends to place our hearts in an incorrect position. There are many individuals who could have reached the shores of destiny years ago, but have not arrived yet due to this issue.

The problem is they decided to only chase after money in their occupations instead of what flooded their hearts with joy, and their spirits with fulfillment. The economic recession from 2007 until now has caused many people to reevaluate their priorities. Millions have discovered their own existence apart from the money they acquire or their occupation. Millions of jobs have been eliminated leaving millions of individuals wondering what happened to the way of life they once knew.

Work Autopsy

The thing that most Americans have failed to realize is that job security does not exist. It is as real as Santa Claus, the Easter Bunny and the Tooth Fairy. Jobs are never permanent, but the education and knowledge we attain will stay with us for life. For many, the primary focus has been on money and material goods. There are so many of people in financial distress right now because they have tried to create and maintain lifestyles their incomes cannot sustain. When debt and unpaid bills rule our minds, it is difficult for us to hear the voice of God. There are too many individuals who have MasterCard as their master instead of God. Many people have been living financially broken and down for years unable to find the strength to stand up again.

In their best selling book The Millionaire Next Door, authors Dr. Thomas J. Stanley and Dr. William Danko listed 7 factors common among people who build financial wealth. I have paraphrased them on page 88.

They do not purchase items outside of their budget
They view their time as valuable and they budget to build wealth
They are not flashy with their purchases and prefer to have financial freedom over trying to impress other people
Their parents did not pay all of their bills once they entered the working world
Their adult children can financially take care of themselves
They understand which investments make them money and which ones cause them to lose it
They chose the correct career path that allowed their gifts and talents to be maximized

Even though Doctor's Stanley and Danko listed choosing the right occupation as their seventh common wealth factor, in my mind its number one. When most people look for work the most important factors they consider are who is hiring and how much will they pay? It is a rarity to hear someone say, what kind of business should I start or how can I best use my gifts and talents to create financial independence?

As I alluded to previously, not everyone is meant to work a blue or white-collar job. There are some of us whose destiny will entail starting our own business. Others may need to go back to school or acquire more training or quality life experience to reach their occupational destiny. Each of us must learn the critical skills needed to think outside of life's box. This book should help with that cause.

The company that you work for was not your dream. It was the dream of its founder. There are millions of Americans unhappily trading in valuable hours of their lives for money every day. Many of them are unhappy with their jobs, the money they make, and the amount of time they spend there daily. Imagine how much happier they would be if they were able to trade in their time for meaning instead.

Numerous others are married to jobs that God drew up the divorce papers on years ago. They have been stuck in bad cases of occupational matrimony in which their gifts and talents have been placated. As the bills pile up around them and the frustration grows within them, they begin to long for the days when their dreams seemed tangible. They resign themselves to feeling that only money itself could truly solve their problems. They fail to answer the following questions.

Why do I work every day?
Why am I working where I work?
Is this the destiny that God has called me to fulfill?
Is this a transition point for me?
What occupation will allow me to be compensated handsomely for doing what I love enough to do for free?

The Cold Reality

Day after day, month after month, and year after year people fail to answer these questions. Others answer the questions but then neglect to apply their solutions. They all simply assume that whatever work they do presently must be the will of God for their lives. Otherwise they would be doing something else. This laboring individual style of thinking would be great if this was 1950 in a city like Detroit, Michigan or Buffalo, New York where jobs were plentiful then. Unfortunately, times are different and with changing times there must be a new school approach.

If a company's financial numbers do not look strong in a fiscal quarter there will be cuts made. If you are not the owner or CEO of the company there is no guaranteeing that you will not be part of these cuts. It does not matter how hard you worked or how many years you have been there.

You are simply a name and a salary listed on a Microsoft Excel spreadsheet to them. In the field of business loyalty is only good if it generates a profit.

Each one of us must learn to listen for and adhere to the call of God within our hearts. For some of you it may say it is your destiny to stick it out at the company; For others it may be to start a small business while you are still employed; For others it may be to go back to school or to start a business while unemployed. I do not know what your personal call is telling you, but I do know that God has your number and will be contacting you soon. Whatever call he places on your life please remember to honor him through your hard and accurate work. Please do not wait until you have a pink slip before you get your financial house in order.

No matter how old you are, it is never too late to take the voyage from security to the shores of destiny. The book of Proverbs chapter 18 verse 16 tells us, "a mans gift makes room for him, and brings him before great men." There is a place right now or in the future where your gift will be needed and admired. Don't be a statistic be a standard bearer. Give your gifts and talents an opportunity to flourish daily.

There are too many people working in mismatched occupations while letting their God given gifts and talents spoil. God will grant us the ability to discern when it is time to make a move. Someone reading this right now the Lord gave you discernment years ago and you still have not moved. The lack of movement has caused some of our gifts and talents to atrophy due to lack of usage.

In order for you to reach your destiny, your gifts and talents must be exercised daily. Sometimes we may work in occupations where our intangible abilities like character and self-respect are finely tuned and built. It becomes a problem however, when we stay in those places long after God has opened up another door for us. Dream living must change from optional to mandatory to see greater happiness in our lives and throughout our nation.

This type of change will not happen until we start listening to the call of God within our hearts by pursuing our passions. Your passions are tied to your purpose for living. When you know your purpose, money doesn't mean much to you. Its importance is diminished. When you let your passions live through the application of your gifts and talents, you will have the combination of money and happiness that millions of people long for.

The laboring way of thinking must be left behind in your past. Money is a means to an end, but not the end. There are so many people who work a minimum of 40 hours per week in areas that do not interest them. They trade in the prime years of their life to earn money to pay expenses. They feel that the life they have crafted is their lot in life and will not get better.

These individuals live their lives dreading Sunday night and praying that Friday comes expeditiously every week. They spend their lives living for the weekend and the paid vacation days sprinkled throughout the calendar. They never take the time to figure out who they are and what they represent.

These individuals work at least 8 hours a day with only their lunch hour breaking up the monotony of their days. God may be calling them to something greater, but they resist because all they know is a life of security and non-risk. These individuals neglect to take the chance to aspire higher. They may have an idea of what their purpose for living may be, but they refuse to probe further because no one has told them they can.

Well, here it is, you can do it. You have permission to follow your dreams. This life is too short not to. It is time to end the life of living below your potential. No one is going to value your happiness more than you will. Each of us has the ability to live our lives to our maximum potential. I know this because our Father has equipped us to do so.

Life is too short to spend it working at jobs and in fields that lack your passion. If you truly do what you love you will never labor a day in our life. The functioning actors that live within their destiny see every day as a new opportunity to do whatever they do best.

In my own life, I went from job to job chasing after the highest salaries available. Even though I made enough money to pay my bills, my work left me feeling unfulfilled. I followed the advice of my wallet and what others wanted me to do instead of listening for what God requested of me. One day I prayed to God to show me what he wanted me to do with my life. He answered me, and now this book is one of the fruits of my function.

There is a place and an occupation that everyone can fit perfectly into. The problem is that too many people fit in where they can instead of figuring out where they truly belong. They spend decades trying to make a living while forgetting to make a life. No one should have to look back on their life with regret especially when it comes to their chosen occupation. They are the places in which we spend the bulk of our lives. How can you go through life depriving yourself of a chance to make a living by doing whatever it is that you love to do?

Working a nine to five job is simply not for everyone and neither is becoming an entrepreneur for that matter. When you let your heart and the call of God within it guide you, it will lead you to where you fit perfectly. When you let your wallet and the call of your bank account lead you, you often find heartache and headache waiting for you. Whether your destiny lies in the corporate world, government, or the private sector, you must make sure that you are the best at whatever you do. Ultimately, we do not work for money or to win awards, but to honor God by doing our very best with the gifts and talents that he has given us.

Chapter 11 Questions

1. Why do I work every day?

_____

_____

_____

_____

2. Who is receiving the maximum benefit from my work?

_____

_____

_____

_____

3. Do I believe that my current occupation is my destiny or a transition point on the way to my destiny?

_____

_____

_____

_____

4. Does my current occupation require me to apply my gifts and talents to their maximum capability?

_____

_____

_____

_____

5. What occupation will allow me to be compensated handsomely for doing what I love enough to do it for free?

_____

_____

_____

_____

Chapter 12

Breaking Free From Debt

I touched on this subject a little bit in the last chapter, but I will now delve a little deeper into it. The time has come for many of us to finally take a hard assessment of our finances. More specifically it is time to get debt free. In the book of Deuteronomy chapter 28 verse 13 it states, "And the Lord will make you the head and not the tail; you shall be above only, and not be beneath, if you heed the commandments of the Lord your God, which I command you today and be careful to observe them." It should be the goal of everyone to meet this goal. Children of God deserve the best that life has to offer, but often many of us are robbed of this opportunity due to debt.

The world is a much different place now than when Moses and the Israelites lived. There were no student loans, credit card, mortgage and other various forms of consumer debt that we face today. In those times people that found themselves in debt were of often sold into slavery. Today the penalties range from decreased credit scores to bankruptcy and other undesired fates in between them. I would agree that sometimes financial struggle can be a part of God's will. It can certainly be a trying time that tests our faith in him and builds our character, but I do not believe it is meant to be a lifelong process. The God I serve does not want his people in long term financial bondage. When financial bondage lingers it becomes our object of focus instead of God and his will for our lives.

In 2012, the shackles of debt do not bind the wrists and ankles of those it afflicts it shackles minds and imprisons spirits. Debt is a form of modern day slavery. The book of Proverbs chapter 22 verse 7 states, "the rich rules over the poor and the borrower is servant to the lender." I do not pretend to be a financial expert but I know a dream thief when I see it and debt fits the bill.

Why You Need To Escape

There are a myriad of reasons that cause people to fall into debt. I have included several of them in the box below.

Medical Expenses
Home Mortgage
Auto Loans
Credit Card Debt
Student Loan Debt

These are several prime examples of debts that are stealing the dreams of millions of Americans every day. They are not the only forms of debt in our society but in my mind they affect the majority of Americans.

I listed several reasons that individuals accumulate debt, but there is one main reason to escape it. That one reason is freedom. The destiny that God has called you to fulfill is more important than any form of debt that I have listed. Debt is temporary and does not deserve the power to destroy your long term future. It may delay the journey to your destiny but denial is not an option. I do not care how you got into debt or how much debt you currently have there is a way to become free. You have to fight through the feelings of guilt, depression and hopelessness.

Escaping debt starts with a plan. That plan must include a debt free mind with the vision of becoming a lender instead of a borrower. The advice that most financial experts have is to start with your smallest debt and eliminate it first. After that most advise consumers to then take the money that was once owed on the first debt and apply it to the next smallest debt. The goal is to eliminate debt to become a saver and investor. Savings will provide financial security for you and your family. Investments offer you the opportunity to have your money work for you. The ability to save and invest allows you the opportunity to open up doors for others. Imagine the lives that can be impacted by what God can do through you. I have no doubt in my mind you can get there.

There is someone reading this right now that knows that debt is keeping them from pursuing the destiny that God has for their life. You have to keep pushing through no matter how impossible escaping debt seems. It does not matter if you are one thousand, ten thousand, one hundred thousand, or a million or more dollars in debt. You can and will overcome it.

Look back over your life and reflect on all the seemingly impossible situations that God brought you through. Know that God did not place the dream within you to allow debt to derail your journey. The greater the debt you face, the greater the pressure you face. These are the times when God does his best work. The book of James chapter 5 verse 16 states, "The effective, fervent prayer of a righteous man avails much."

Pressure has the power to burst pipes, but it can also produce diamonds. Will your dreams splatter due to debt or will they sparkle due to you overcoming it? In the book of Matthew chapter 17 verse 20 Jesus states, "Because of your unbelief; for assuredly, I say to you, if you have faith as a mustard seed, you will say to this mountain, 'Move from here to there,' and it will move; and nothing will be impossible for you." That verse lets me know that when we exercise our faith God will strengthen us to do what seems impossible.

In the book of Deuteronomy chapter 8 verse 18 it states, "And you shall remember the Lord your God, for it is He who gives you the power to get wealth, that He may establish his covenant which He swore to your fathers, as it is this day." That verse mentions nothing about God giving us the power to accumulate debt so that we will live depressed and defeated. God grants us the power to do his will on this earth. There is someone out there right now that God has appointed to help you turn your situation around. Make it your mission to find out who that person is. It could be someone that you know personally that has been through a similar situation. Your solution could be a financial book by Cedric Dukes or Suzy Orman or another financial expert. There are also debt consolidation companies that can help put you on the road to financial freedom.

You have to picture yourself debt free before you can get there. See your debts as perishable with a short shelf life and a fast approaching expiration date. Debt has sunken the dreams of so many people. Your dreams will not be its next victim. The biggest key to your success will be the Holy Spirit. I will talk more in depth about the Holy Spirit in chapter 17. The Holy Spirit will guide and direct you to success. It will give you ideas that will enable your breakthrough. With financial education and the assistance of God's Holy Spirit you will be debt free. It will not come overnight but you will get there in due time.

Chapter 12 Questions

1. Is debt delaying or denying my destiny?

_____

_____

_____

_____

2. Do I believe that I can become debt free?

_____

_____

_____

_____

3. Is it my goal to become a lender instead of a borrower?

_____

_____

_____

_____

PART THREE

Wednesday

THE MID POINT TO DESTINY

Chapter 13

Overnight Success Takes Years Of Work

There is no such thing as instant success, it does not exist. If becoming successful was just as simple as taking a magic pill the pharmacies around the world would always be busy. For many of us the destinies that God has for our lives may be as little as a few months away from fruition. For others it will take several more years. The key is being able to thank God as if our success has already happened.

If someone knew that God's call for their life was for them to become a Medical Doctor, Medical school would be a prerequisite. They simply could not wake up one day and decide that they were a Doctor without first completing the necessary requirements. To make the move from the land of security to the shores of destiny there must be a period of training. The training precedes the full transition.

There are a great number of people who would like to become business owners, but have never learned how to be great employees first. How can you truly expect God to transition your life if you have not proven yourself worthy of it? Your level of worthiness is proven by your ability to do great things no matter where you are. It is also proven in your drive to be great when mediocrity is the most popular thing surrounding you. It is your pattern of excellence that places you on the road of greatness.

Tyler Perry

During the transition period to our destiny our character is built and made strong. The tough path will make us truly appreciate the ability to revel in our destiny once we reach it. If proof is what you seek, look at the life of entertainment mogul Tyler Perry. Perry struggled through many years of heartache, disappointment, and uncertainty before finally hitting pay dirt with his 1998 stage play, I Know I've Been Changed. He held on to the calling that God placed in his heart, even though it didn't seem at times like he would ever reach his destiny.

Through times of homelessness, odd jobs and a lack of family support he pushed forward with his dreams. There were nights when he didn't know if he could make them a reality. The only way that he was able to keep pushing forward at his lowest points was due to God's hands being on his back through it all.

When God puts the call of destiny in us he then places his hands on our backs to ensure that we do not fall in our toughest hours. It is incumbent upon us to earnestly do the dirty work in laying the foundation for our destiny.

Doing the dirty work ensures that once we reach our destiny, we will not forget who made it possible for us to get there. It would have been easy for Mr. Perry to quit when the dirty work got hard, but thank God for keeping the calling alive in him through it all. We all have a little Tyler Perry in us, but it will only reveal itself if we obey God's call for our lives and commit our lives to reaching our destiny.

Kurt Warner

Back in 1999, one of the most improbable stories of success played out in St. Louis, Missouri. Kurt Warner, a 28-year-old former grocery store stock boy was given a chance to quarterback the National Football League's St. Louis Rams. When projected starter Trent Green went down with a season ending knee injury, Coach Dick Vermeil turned to the unknown Warner.

Up until that point the previous 5 years for Warner were a complete whirlwind. He went undrafted out of Northern Iowa University in 1994, but was signed by the Green Bay Packers. Not long after being signed, he was released by the Packers and faced an uncertain future. He subsequently got married and landed a job as a stock clerk at a Hy-Vee grocery store just to pay the bills.

Right then and there he could have easily given up and told himself, "even though I possess the God given ability to play football at the highest level, it doesn't matter, I will live out my life stocking shelves." He knew that God placed all the gifts and talents within him to succeed. All he needed was an opportunity. He did the necessary dirty work by continuing to refine his ability to throw footballs. He spent every day he could preparing himself for a future that seemed improbable. His hard work eventually paid off, and the Iowa Barnstormers of the Arena Football League signed him.

Warner played well enough in Iowa that the NFL's St. Louis Rams decided to give him an opportunity to try out. They sent him to NFL Europe, which at the time was the minor league for the NFL. In 1999, after a year in Europe, Warner joined the Rams and was elevated to the starting quarterback when Trent Green went down with an injury. As many of you know, Warner led St. Louis to a Super Bowl title that year while earning the MVP trophy for himself. It is not likely that Warner would have been able to lead Green Bay to a title when he was first signed in 1994. It took 5 years of dirty work, and the right set of circumstances for him to reach the destiny that God had for him.

Both Perry and Warner faced times when they were not sure if they would ever make it to their destiny. They both held on and as a result, the world is made better with their heartwarming inspirational stories. God allows us to go through processes so that we never forget that he alone was the one who brought us through them. In any area of life, when we take care of the work, God will work out the circumstances.

Not all of us will become entertainment moguls or NFL most valuable players, but we all can become whatever it is that God destined for us to become. If overnight success really did exist, we would all believe that we were successful because of our own doing or luck instead of God's favor. Something not earned is nothing worth having. Trying to make it to the shores of destiny without putting in the prerequisites is a journey doomed for failure. When we make it a point to practice our craft, God will help us perfect it.

Chapter 13 Questions

1. Does reaching my destiny seem like an impossible concept?

_____

_____

_____

_____

2. Would I prefer to earn my destiny or have it given to me?

_____

_____

_____

_____

3. Do I have enough patience to do the dirty work to reach my destiny?

_____

_____

_____

_____

4. What steps must I take right now to fulfill the prerequisites of my destiny?

_____

_____

_____

_____

Chapter 14

No Quitting On The Pathway To Destiny

There is no need to give up once God puts a calling in our hearts. For whomever God calls he also equips, to fulfill the calling. So many people have let God's dreams for them drown in the sea of mediocrity on the path to destiny. They leave the land of security full of ambition with the fire of success burning within them, but they fail to sustain it. Many of them have allowed job cuts, the death of relatives, bad relationships, critics and negative thinking to allow their dreams to drown.

Then there are the individuals who are strong enough to withstand outside forces, but fail to win the battle within their minds. They constantly get in the way of their potential future by letting elements such as discouragement, despair and depression prevent them from reaching God's destination for them. They let the three d's of disappointment lock them into lives featuring inaction and procrastination as their calling cards.

Fighting Procrastination

Webster's dictionary defines procrastination as putting off doing something until later. I define it as a close relative of quitting. For millions of people later arrived and they still neglected to make any movements. This shows obedience to their problems and disobedience to God's instructions. There are so many people that God placed visions full of promise and destiny in them years ago and they still have not moved yet. Many are struggling with discouragement, despair and depression wondering what might have been if they would have acted sooner.

There are many of us who know that if we had listened and acted upon the call of God in our hearts we could have avoided unnecessary heartache and pain. Whenever we disobey God, our lives have a tendency to become uncomfortable. The reason that we need to take action is simple. Each of us represents a problem solver for someone else.

There is someone out in the world right now that needs what God has placed within you to share. It could be a business innovation, a song, a ministry, an invention, a book, or even an idea for film or television. Only you know what it is in you. So many of us say to ourselves, I know that God is leading me to do_____ but I am just not ready today. We then say we will wait until next week, which becomes next month, which then manifests into a year or more of inaction.

Do we ever stop to think about all the people we deprive of what God has placed in us during our periods of inaction. All the lives going un-blessed from us not putting to use what God has placed in us. Think about how we could be living out our destiny by simply following the call of God.

All we have to do is take things one step at a time. There is nothing wrong with taking baby steps toward our future. The problem is when we continue to take baby steps when God is imploring and blazing the trail for us to take giant leaps. This happens when we procrastinate and delay our destiny for no good reason. If we can go to jobs we detest every day on time, there is no excuse to be late when God calls us to action.

Aretha Franklin and Fantasia Barrino

For some of us it may not be an issue with procrastination that has us our dreams drowning in the sea of mediocrity. There are many people who have allowed the vicissitudes of life to anchor them into quitting on the call that God has given them. Some individuals may have children before they were financially ready and use it as an excuse for not reaching or attempting to reach their goals. I say take a look at the lives of Aretha Franklin and Fantasia Barrino.

These two women faced difficult circumstances in their lives and refused to quit. They knew that God put callings within each of their lives and both determined that their destinies would not be denied. They didn't allow being young single mothers sink the calling of God on their lives. They used their situation as a motivational springboard to their destiny, instead of an anchor to sink them into failure. Instead of saying I can't make it because of my children, they said I have no choice but to make it for my children.

You may not have the rich vocal precision to burn up the charts, but never forget that God has placed his specific calling within each of our hearts. Music may not be your gift, but we all have a gift that if cultivated and nurtured will land us living out our purpose on the shores of our destiny.

Dave Thomas and Bill Gates

Maybe for you it was not becoming a young parent that in your mind excludes you from your destiny. For you it could possibly be the lack of a high school or college education. Look no further than your local Wendy's restaurant or any Microsoft application on your computer. Neither Wendy's founder Dave Thomas nor Microsoft founder Bill Gates let the lack of a high school diploma or a college degree respectively prevent them from reaching their God gifted destiny. Just imagine how different the world would be without Wendy's hamburgers or Microsoft computer software applications. These gentlemen did not let a lack of formal education prevent them from living their dreams.

When God puts a call within your heart, the world cannot disconnect the line. We are the only ones with the ability to not answer or hang up on the call. When we keep the line open it allows God to give us his fail proof instructions to reach his appointed destiny for us. I understand that for most of our dreams to be realized, we will need to possess varying levels of higher formal education. Each of us must determine the prerequisites for our individual dreams and meet them.

Loss

For others it could be the loss of a loved one or something you value that has put your dreams on hold. It is imperative that you cling to the fact that when someone or something passes away, there is always a rebirth to take the place of the former. It is human nature for our losses to knock us down, but it is divine nature for us to rise up again. God will not allow times of dark clouds and rain to permeate with us without sunshine succeeding it. In the book of Psalms chapter 30 verse 5 it states, "for his anger is but for a moment, His favor is for life; Weeping may endure for a night, but joy comes in the morning."

Whenever there are dark clouds and rain in our lives, sunshine and bright skies will follow them. In the same manner as plants, the times of dark clouds and rain force us to grow. We grow so that when the sunshine comes we can blossom and become radiant examples of God's greatness. Times of joy will follow times of pain, it is the natural flow of nature. God knows that we hurt when we suffer losses in this world. No matter who we are we will eventually lose someone or something that we love. For some of us these losses have tethered us to the dark clouds of discouragement, despair and depression. Each one of us handles our losses differently.

At some point however, each of us that suffers must make the decision to survive. We must muster the strength to carry on with our lives. As harsh as it sounds, when we are deluged in our deepest levels of hurt the clock will not stop for us. The world will still rotate around us even when we feel that pain and suffering have been our only company.

In those times we must lean on God and take comfort in the fact that our race moves on. We must not forget the loss of a loved one or something we treasure, but we must pay our best tributes by continuing to strive for the destinies that God has called us to. When these tough times strike we must employ our faith into action.

In the book of Proverbs chapter 3 verse 5 it states, "Trust in the Lord with all your heart, and lean not on your own understanding; In all your ways acknowledge him and he shall direct your paths." This lets us know that things may happen that we do not understand, but we still must trust that God knows exactly what he is doing.

The individuals in this life who win God's way learn how to turn adversity into fuel to propel them to their destiny. There is no heart that God cannot heal and no void that he cannot fill. You must not let loss keep you permanently away from the destiny that God has placed in you. Know that when God allows one door to close, he will open up a vault of blessings that you could not have imagined. Losses will hurt but you must not allow them to permanently cripple your dreams. God is always in charge even when the problems that we face attempt to rule our minds.

Job Loss

There is someone reading this book that has recently lost their job. You find your life at the intersection of where do I go road and how do I get there boulevard. I can assure

110

you that God has not forgotten about you. I may not be able to fill up your pantry with food or pay your bills, but I can offer you hope. This is no shame in losing your job especially with today's current economic situation. You are not alone in your struggles.

I know the humbling reality of walking into a state unemployment office and having to ask the state government to temporarily assist you financially. I have been in that situation and was able to get through it with the help of God, a strong mind and supportive people around me.

A Bible verse that helped me during my time of uncertainty was Psalm 40 verses 1-2. It reads, "I waited patiently for the Lord; And he inclined to me, and heard my cry. He also brought me up out of a horrible pit, out of the miry clay, and set my feet upon a rock, and established my steps." When King David wrote this he was in a period of distress and knew that only God could bring him out of it. The God of King David is still at work today.

You may have lost your job, but could soon be landing near your destiny. God may have been leading you in a direction that you may have been resisting due to your job. Now that the job is in your past, God could be forcing you to move into the position he has designated for you to be. Allow your mind to be open to the imagination of God.

This is not a time to let depression and negative thoughts rule your mind. It is the time to discover who you are again and where your passion resides. Please hold on to your faith in God. The same God that saw King David through his troubles will see you through as well. Take the time to search your heart and seek his word, there you will find the answer that you seek. While searching for your answer within, still take time to search for another legitimate tangible income source to pay your expenses while building your dream. Use whatever free time you have to construct your dreams. Jobs may come and go but your passion and gifts will never leave you.

Impatience

Someone reading this may be ready to quit on the call of their destiny due to impatience. You allow a red sea of impatience and the uncertainty of success to make you quit before reaching your destination. In the Bible the Israelites reached the Promised Land, a land that was first revealed to Abraham. His descendant Moses led them to the doorstep, but his descendant Joshua fulfilled the promise.

For a great number of us our ancestors had dreams that they were unable to fulfill in their lifetime. They went to their graves with a feeling that one day a descendent of theirs would carry out the promise. They understood that the promise that God gave them did not come with a specific date of completion. For many of us our parents and grandparents were not able to fulfill those promises. We must have the attitude that the buck will stop with us. We must make up our minds to take the key that God placed within us and use it to unlock the promise.

The problem is when we know that we have the key, but the promise of God is not presenting itself expeditiously enough for us. We forget that the promises of God happen on his time not ours. It may take years before you reach your destiny, but you must not quit in the mean time. I will talk more about God's timing in chapter 19.

It took the Israelites 40 years to make it to the Promised Land, but nevertheless they made it. When we obey God's instructions he will make sure that we reach our destiny at the perfect time. It may not come when we want it, but please trust that the timing will be right. We must be patient with God, for he knows what is best for each of us.

The promise may have been revealed to our ancestors over a century ago, but the only way that the promise can be fulfilled is for us to not quit while waiting on God's timing. You may not be as ready as you think you are. You must learn not to quit simply because you do not know the exact date that God has appointed for your arrival at destiny. It is your responsibility to hold onto your hope even when your destiny may seem out of reach. You must stay prayed up and striving for greatness in all things in the meantime. If you continue doing your part, God will show up on time ready to guide you to the shores of destiny.

Mental Warfare

There are also many of us who quit on the call of destiny simply because we talk ourselves out of it. We were fired up leaving the land of security and let our mind sink us halfway to our destiny. Someone reading this is currently facing this set of circumstances. You allow thoughts such as I can't make it, God did not call me, I am too young, I am too old, I am not special and I do not have what it takes to infiltrate your mind. As I said earlier, whomever God calls he also equips. He equips us with a full compliment of the gifts and talents we will need to reach our destiny. He orchestrated the process for your gifts, talents and destiny to meet with you acting as the facilitator of the meeting.

It is untrue to believe that God would decide to waste his time creating and equipping a person he did not have special plans for. Don't get to a point halfway to your destiny and let negative thoughts deter you. If God had no plans for you to reach your destiny, he would not have placed the calling in your heart in the first place.

Please do not let self get in the way of what God has designed for your life. When you win the battle of the mind you remove a cloud obstructing the view of your future destination. God created us to propel with precision and not be sunk by our thoughts. Even when times get rough, quitting on the journey to your destiny is not an option. God has put too much stock in you for you to quit.

If God granted us the gift of life, the least we owe him is giving ourselves an opportunity to complete the mission he assigned to our lives. Instead of mission aborted we must strive for mission completed instead. Quitting may be our choice, but completing our mission is God's will. It is never over until God says it is over and it is not over until we complete the course.

Chapter 14 Questions

1. Have I quit on reaching my destiny in the middle of my journey?

_____

_____

_____

_____

2. What will it take for me to get back on the path heading in the direction of my destiny?

_____

_____

_____

_____

3. Are the problems that I face more important than following what God has instructed me to do?

_____

_____

_____

_____

4. Is my faith stronger than the circumstances that I face?

_____

_____

_____

_____

Chapter 15

Don't Bury The Treasure Without Leaving A Map

If your life suddenly ended today, would you ask God to allow you to go back to earth? If you did, what reasons would you give? The truth is people like you and I are dying every day. They are tall and short. They are young and old. They are famous, infamous and anonymous. By virtue of you reading this book, and by benefit of the grace and mercy of God, you were not one of those people.

There are two things that life guarantees to all. They consist of death and taxes, as many of us know all too well. As our taxes must be paid by April 15th of every year, our dates of death carry an unknown date of fruition. A lot of people go through their lives as if they will never run out of time. We hear stories of celebrities or we see someone we know pass away, and it jars us for a moment. We briefly reflect and then continue our lives as if it were business as usual. We live that way until we receive the confirmation of another person leaving the earth.

In all honesty, none of us has a clue when it will be our time to leave this earth we call home. Most people hope to be able to get old and watch their grandchildren blossom like flowers. This hope is not guaranteed however. The book of Psalms chapter 90 verse 10 tells us, "The days of our lives are seventy years; and if by reason of strength they are eighty years, yet their boast is only labor and sorrow, for it is soon cut off, and we fly away." The Bible may promise us seventy or eighty years of living, but one look at the obituary section of our local newspapers paints a much bleaker picture.

It has been said for many years that the richest places on earth are not banks or stock exchanges, but graveyards. There will come a time when we will exit stage left and the curtain will close on our lives. Will you be proud of your production? Will you have lived your life in the land of false security with your dreams held captive by fear and a lack of knowledge? Will your time run out while you are making your way to the shores of destiny, striving to make your dreams a reality? Finally, will you have lived and enjoyed life living within your calling in the land of destiny? What will it take for you to be able to look back and consider your mission completed.

The Gift of Life

So many people base their self worth and legacy on the strength of their monetary net worth. Our true self worth and legacy are measured in the number of lives we touch. When we pass away, the money that we leave here will eventually be spent by someone else. It can easily be disinherited and wasted by those we leave behind. On the other hand the number of lives we touch will be infinite in number and will never disinherit itself from the world. It is better to have lived a life rich with love and respect as opposed to monetary riches.

There is no person living today who knows the exact day and hour when they will leave this place we call earth. Too many people take the gift of life that God has given us for granted. Each person is an integral part of God's plan. Living our lives and not striving for our calling is a wasted mission. We get so busy living our lives that we neglect to hear the voice of God. The reason God blesses us, is to prove his glory through the example of our lives. We are also to be a positive example of how to live for those around us. It is critical that we use what God has given us to be blueprints and not carbon copies. We must understand that people die every day and that none of us are immortal.

Treasure Chest

For many of the people in our lives we may be the only positive blueprints they know personally. Our society idolizes entertainment stars, politicians and athletes, but how many of us know them personally. We may cheer for them, but we do not know them. The people in our lives do not know them either, but they do know us.

I had my own personal blueprint he was my maternal grandfather Willie Moore. He was born on a Mississippi farm in the early 20th century. Times were hard for him growing up mud poor, having to share crop on old plantation fields to survive. Through God's grace he made it through those tough times.

In the early 1940's he was drafted to fight in WWII. He served this great nation and returned to Mississippi in 1946. He then followed the calling in his heart and moved to Detroit, Michigan that same year. He took a job at Ford Motor Company and worked for over 30 years, living his American dream.

By the time I was born in the early 1980's, he was living the good life. He and my grandmother had already raised three adult children, and he was retired living comfortably on his Ford pension. It seemed as if his mission was completed. This was not good enough for God however. God called him to do one more project.

His last task was to make sure that he poured into me all the treasure (wisdom) that existed within him. He took me everywhere he went and showed me what it took to be the person that God called him to be. He taught me how to love and respect others, to be a person of excellent character and to live as if God was watching.

In our last conversation, he let me know that he was proud of the man that I became as a result of his influence.

He implored me to carry on and share my treasure with others. My grandfather decided that letting the treasure die trapped inside of him was unacceptable. Even though he departed this earth several years ago, the treasure of my grandfather still lives today through my work and within me as well. He decided that he would not die without giving away the treasure that was given to him. He gave it to me and it is my responsibility to share it with the world.

Where is the Treasure?

The richest people in the world are not CEO's of billion dollar corporations or celebrities. They are the people around us who are willing to share what God has blessed them with. They are the treasure givers or actors emeritus as I referred to them earlier. There are so many ideas for new inventions, new books, and new businesses that are buried in cemeteries with their owners.

My friends, be like my grandfather and use what God has put in you to bless others. Do not go to the grave with unfinished business and regret. Go to the grave empty with promises filled and your life assignment completed. There is no better day than today to enrich the lives of others with your treasure. Let your life be a living testimony of the right way to go. It is never too late to make the necessary changes to make it possible.

God gives us an opportunity every day that we live to impart wisdom, hope and knowledge in others. There is no use in waiting until you get old to begin this process. As I said earlier, no day is guaranteed to any of us. People are alive and well today and dead and gone in the same day. The only thing that separated us from being in their shoes is the grace of God.

My grandfather will never be in the history books, or on the national news, but it's ok. He didn't live to be famous or to garner attention for all of the positive things he did. He was and still is my favorite celebrity. Your treasure is meant to be shared and not hoarded. Be the shining blueprint in a land of carbon copies. When you die what will you be remembered for? How long will you be remembered?

Impact on this earth will last several lifetimes but money will fade away. Do not die being a person pregnant with potential. In the words of Les Brown, it should be the goal of everyone to live full and die empty. The only way that we can truly live full is to reach our destiny and send a map to help others reach where we reside. We were not created to be stingy hoarders, but cheerful givers. It is a crime to let your treasure tarnish in the graveyard. Let it shine for the world to enjoy and God will make sure you are rewarded properly.

Sharing The Treasure

When we share our treasure it is important that we do not force the information upon our intended recipient. If we try to force it upon them, our precious words and actions of wisdom will not be absorbed by those we intend to share it with. A person has to be willing to learn from us to receive the true benefit of our message. In the same manner that a person can only change when they are ready to, the same goes for learning as well. God will lead us to the exact person who needs our treasure at the right time. It could be a family member, friend, co-worker or even a person we meet on the street.

Receiving The Treasure

If a person is willing to share their treasure with us, it is important that we have an open mind and a receptive heart. By simply listening to and watching the person offering their treasure, it can potentially save us a huge amount of future heartache. There is absolutely nothing wrong with learning in 5 minutes what it may have taken someone else 10 years or more to grasp. This is an example of their hard work paying us dividends in the form of our smart work.

Talking to someone who has went through what you are going through or done something in life that you aspire to do is invaluable. Take what you need from them and filter out what you will not need. This kind of knowledge cannot be duplicated in history books or on the Internet. It is then incumbent upon you to take the treasure that you are being given and someday deposit it into someone else. We all have to take our own path to our destiny, but a proven blueprint is a resource not to be taken for granted.

Chapter 15 Questions

1. Am I proud of my life thus far? If not what can I do to improve it?

_____

_____

_____

_____

2. If I died today what would I leave unfinished?

_____

_____

_____

_____

3. What is my legacy as of today?

_____

_____

_____

_____

4. Am I open to sharing my treasure with others?

_____

_____

_____

_____

5. Am I open to receiving treasure from other people?

_____

_____

_____

_____

Chapter 16

You Can't Make It Alone

Even though our journeys in life are individual, no one can reach their destiny without the assistance of others. Our existence on this earth can only be as good as the people we surround ourselves with. Just as it takes the help of a village to raise a child, it takes the help of a village for us to reach our destiny. It truly takes a team effort. Look all around you and determine who is in your corner, and are supportive of the dreams within your heart. If you have people around you hoping that you fail, obviously it is not wise to listen to their opinions.

In my life I have to thank God for the support of my family, especially my mother. Even when they did not know exactly how I would make it to my destiny, they sowed seeds of positivity into my life. They always encouraged me to set the bar high and to accomplish my goals. People do not need to know exactly what you are doing, but nonetheless their support is important. To truly make it to your destiny and enjoy life there, it is imperative that you have your priorities in order. Below I have listed what I feel are the best order for priorities in life.

| 1. Relationship with God |
| 2. Relationship with Family and Friends |
| 3. Life's Work (Occupation) |

By placing your relationship with God first it allows you to have a visual order for how your life should be lived. Everything else follows in order after God, because without him nothing would be possible. He is the one who has blessed us with our loving families and friends, and the ability to earn a living by applying the gifts and talents that he blessed us with. The items listed on page 122 must be in the proper order for you to truly live as God has called you to. When you do this you allow the support of God, and that of your family and friends to ultimately enrich your life's work.

Millions of people in this world today are placing their careers and life work above everything else, and are forgetting God, and letting their families suffer as a result of their lack of proper priority. There is nothing wrong with working hard but it is a problem when we give everything we have to our jobs and have nothing left to share with God and our families. My personal priority list is very similar to the branches of our government here in the United States listed below.

US Government

1. Executive Branch
2. Judicial Branch
3. Legislative Branch

The job of the Executive Branch is to preserve, protect and defend the constitution, and to protect the laws of our country. They are made up of the President and his cabinet. The job of the Judicial Branch is to judge and rule as to whether laws have been kept or broken. They act as interpreters of the law. They are made up of judges and represent our court system. Finally, the Legislative branch makes the laws, controls the federal budget and is made up of Congress.

Just as the President and his cabinet represent the Executive Branch of this country, God and his angels represent the Executive Branch of our very lives. They are responsible for giving us a center to look to in maintaining or balancing our priorities in life. Our families represent the Judicial Branch, they generally keep us grounded and guide us with their compass of love and morality. They usually let us know when we are wrong and applaud us when we are right. Our careers represent the Legislative Branch in our lives. They are where our work is rewarded usually with money and the satisfaction of a job well done.

Just take a look around at the car you drive or the home or apartment where you live. Did one person build these things? I highly doubt it. Just as a designer has a singular vision of how a car or how a house should be built, they cannot be created without the assistance of others.

Our lives are very similar to this process. We have the vision and chart the blueprints for our lives. Our family and friends represent the screws, nuts and bolts that hold us together. God represents the foundation or chassis that everything is built on top of. No one on this earth can make it anywhere worth going to without the support of others.

Presidents and other elected officials cannot be elected alone. They need people to vote for them. Athletes are paid as a result of fan attendance at sporting events. Recording artists are able to make a living as a result of fans buying their music and concert tickets. Even you in your present occupation are paid as a result of someone paying your company for the work you do. Each of these examples drives home the point that none of us can make it alone.

The Importance of Keeping God 1st

Scores of people place their life's work above God and their families. There are countless families and friendships strained daily due to individuals devoting all of their energy and resources into work related ventures. These individuals give so much of themselves to the trade that brings them money that their families and friends are left shortchanged.

There are also individuals who devote so much of themselves to their trade and to their families and friends, that they shortchange their relationship with God. Many of us forget who gave us the ability to apply our trades, and supplied us with family and friends to love. Without your relationship with God as your top priority, your straight paths will become crooked. The indirectness of your paths will reveal themselves in the form of disharmony within your life.

When you learn to acknowledge God above any and all things it helps guide your decision making and allows you to evaluate your life from the proper perspective. The Lord knows what is best for you even when you may not agree with his assessment. In the book of Psalms chapter 37 verses 23-26 it states, "The steps of a good man are ordered by the Lord, and He delights in his way. Though he fall, he shall not be utterly cast down; For the Lord upholds him with His hand. I have been young, and now am old; Yet I have not seen the righteous forsaken, Nor his descendants begging for bread. He is ever merciful, and lends; And his descendants are blessed."

This passage illustrates to us the importance of keeping our relationship with God as our top priority. When life becomes difficult and the journey to your destiny is unclear, you must know that God has you covered always. God is always looking to bless you and does not want you to drag through life living in a downtrodden state.

Many times we may suffer unnecessary discord in our lives due to not following the steps that God has ordered us to take. Others may follow the ordered steps, but may not be walking in them at the approximate time that God has ordered the steps to be taken. The great thing about God is even when we may not follow the ordered steps, or walk in them at the right time, he does not forsake us. When it seems that we have fallen, he is there to lift us up and place us back where we need to be. All we must do is communicate with him through prayer, and he will fill our hearts with his divine instructions.

There is no way to make it to the shores of destiny without having a personal relationship with God, and keeping your relationship with him first. In the book of Mark chapter 12 verse 30 Jesus states, "And you shall love the Lord your God with all your heart, with all your soul, with all your mind, and with all your strength. This is the first commandment."

Jesus here illustrated the utter importance of keeping our relationship with God first above all things. The direction that God gives us is for us only. There is no need to phone a friend or a psychic hotline, for God has granted us his Holy Spirit to use as our guiding mechanism. The Holy Spirit resides inside each of us who are open to receiving it. Keeping God first allows his divine instructions to flow freely from Heaven without interruption.

Importance of Keeping Family & Friends 2nd

Ranking behind God, your second priority should be family and friends. Family and friends are the people that God has blessed you with to help fill in the complete picture of your life. These are the earthly people supplied by Heaven to help you reach your destiny. They represent your respite of peace when the world around you becomes a cauldron of calamity.

A main reason that family ranks over occupation is because they love you not for what you may appear to be, but for who you truly are. The chemical composition of your blood is denser than money or your occupation could ever be. The deposits within the love account your family and close friends provide to you can never be over drafted. Their purpose is to also grant you love without conditions, keep you honest, and be beacons of support in your life.

Unfortunately, many of us take these people for granted and allow our work time to take precedent over quality time spent with our family and close friends. Many of us assume that our family and friends will be there forever, and that we can shoehorn them into our lives whenever we have extra time. We give our occupation our best and those closest to us whatever we have left. This method of thinking has caused the breakup of many marriages and fractured relationships with children who only know us through stories told about us, and picture frames displaying our faces.

For some, the breakthrough moment happens when they are served with divorce papers, or a friend or family member passes away. Those trying situations become times of introspection and detailed life evaluation. I implore whoever reads this to not let things reach those tragic points before you analyze and reorganize the priorities of your life.

Even if you may live far away from your family and/or friends, visit them whenever you are able, and call them to show them that you care about them. Do not allow yourself to become the person someday looking back on their life arrested with regret for making your work life a top priority over your family and friends. In truth our families and friends do not care how much money we make, or how great outsiders feel we are at our occupations. What matters to them is the fact that we give them quality time, and large quantities of love for good measure. Our families and friends tell us things that we may not want to hear, but definitely need to hear.

Representing God at Home

There are tons of people who put on a great face at their occupations leaving their co-workers with the impression that they are God's gift to mankind. Many of these same people go home and treat their family and friends as if they were third class citizens. Maybe this is you or someone you may know. They must learn to see their families and friends as blessings from God, not menial servants to be lorded over with abuse and neglect.

Dr. Phillip McGraw says "it is my mission to make sure that if my wife was in a stadium full of women, she would know that no other woman there is treated behind closed doors better than her." This edict is not just limited to spouses but extends to everyone else we consider dear to us. If more of us made this our mission the quality of our home lives would improve.

It amazes me that many of us expect Heaven to bless us when we keep hell raised in our home life. We act like Christ in public and impersonate the devil behind closed doors. It should be the goal of each of us to permit the light of God to radiate within our beings at all times. We must strive to treat people better than we would like to be treated, especially within our own homes.

Many people are forfeiting their opportunity to reach their destiny simply due to the manner in which they treat the people closest to them. I understand that no one is perfect myself included, but if peace is absent in our homes, how can we truly become all that God has destined for us to become? It should be your duty to treat those closest to you with reverence and the utmost respect. Having loving family and friends is a divine gift that many people take for granted every day.

If you died today, what would your legacy reflect tomorrow? Would the people outside of your home view you as a saint and your loved ones view you as Satan? The answer to this question is best reflected in the impression that your character leaves on the individuals you encounter. Being respectful and kind to others, especially your loved ones costs you nothing but rewards you with a legacy to be proud of.

Even though the public may not see how we treat those closest to us, God sees it. It is from him whom all blessings flow, and from him who also possesses the power to block the flow of blessings as well. This happens when our words and actions bring dishonor to him in the manner that we treat others, especially to those whom he has placed into our lives as family members and friends. If a camera were in your home 24 hours a day, would you be proud of what it captured? If your answer is no, then there must be work done to improve the situation.

The Value of Friends

It has been said that if a person were truly able to gain at least one or two great friends in this world, it would be an accomplishment. The people that we consider to be our friends should be treated with the same level of love and respect as our family members. After all they are the family members that we get to pick. For some of us our friends may be closer to us than many of our family members. Webster's dictionary defines friend as a person whom one knows well and is fond of; an ally, supporter or sympathizer. We must be friendly to our friends because they represent a significant portion of our support system.

Imagine if Jesus had come to earth and never made any true friends. Would there be a St. Peter, and Apostle Paul or a Christian church spread around our modern world. Even Jesus knew the value of friendship. His friends on earth spread his message that continues to reign supreme here 20 centuries after his life on earth. Without the assistance of St. Peter and the 11 other chief apostles would this have truly been possible.

Without his friends promoting his agenda, there would be no Bibles to instruct us on how to live, or stories to provide us with inspiration and understanding in times of uncertainty. In the book of John chapter 15 verses 13-15 Jesus states, "Greater love has no one than this, than to lay down one's life for his friends. You are my friends if you do whatever I command you. No longer do I call you servants, for a servant does not know what his master is doing; but I have called you friends, for all things that I heard from My Father I have made known to you."

Imagine if Jesus would have treated his friends with disdain and disrespect, just how hard would they have been willing to work with and for him? If he did not treat his friends well, then they would not have remained his friends for very long. The same applies for us today if we do not treat our friends as they deserve to be treated. If we refuse to make time for them or treat them well, then our relationships with them cannot be considered true friendship. They become personally convenient associations instead. Who will help you promote your message? Who are your true friends? If you feel that you have no true friends, always remember that Jesus Christ is a friend to the friendless.

Our relationships with God and with our families ultimately contribute to the success of our life's work. In the city of Pittsburgh, PA, the Allegheny and Monongahela Rivers confluence to form the Ohio River. Our lives are similar to this aquatic connection. The relationships we form with God and our family and friends are best represented in our life's work. The way we behave outside of our homes gives others a glimpse at what the foundations of our individual lives are. If God is truly the number one priority in your life the proof will be reflected in the way in which you treat others. It will also reveal itself by unveiling the level of sincerity within your motives.

The Benefits of Proper Order and Balance

When God and our family and friends are placed in the proper order, we choose to represent them with measured pride and honor daily. They equip us with a sense of purpose to be our best every day. When a person who keeps God first place in their life walks into a room, a feeling of bright positive energy accompanies them. Conversely a person without God in first place carries a darker heavier energy. They look haggard from carrying the weight of the world on their shoulders.

These individuals lack the symbolism of peace in their inner spirits. Many of them feel lost and lack a sense of purpose and direction for their lives. They believe that the money they make is what defines their life. These individuals become enraptured by their work titles. They feel that they alone are responsible for the blessings that God has bestowed upon them.

Many of them act as if they are God in the flesh. Their relationship with God and their families have been demoted on their pecking order of priorities in favor of their occupation, money and titles. Still they have a level of emptiness that they can't seem to explain. On the inside they feel disjointed and do not know why.

They may not truly be able to understand what they are missing until they observe someone with their priorities in the proper order. They wonder to themselves, how in the world can the other person live with their life in a properly balanced existence? The improperly balanced person then realizes that their life has been improperly prioritized and lacked both peace and clarity.

A person with proper priority balance goes through their life recognizing that they are always one person away from a life-altering blessing. These individuals not only recognize it, but they live in a way that reflects that belief. They understand that without God's assistance there would be no life's work for them to apply their trades at. They also have grasped the notion that without family and friends, there would be no one to share their failures and triumphs with either.

Our life's work should be done to honor God, our family and friends and us as well. Everywhere we go in this world we represent each of those four elements. When we meet people in our daily lives, we may be the only representative of God they can visually see. We may also be the only representatives of our family or close circle of friends. For many of us the lack of proper priority balance is hindering our voyage to destiny. There is no one else that can determine for you what your top priorities in life should be, or the order of their ranking. You are the sole determining force with the singular power to make that decision.

It may be possible to gain what the world refers to as success, but without proper priority balance it will be both fleeting and unfulfilling. It would be the equivalent of building a sparkling edifice on top of quicksand. The building may look beautiful, and may hold steady for a little while, but it will eventually fall apart. The building can never be built to withstand the test of time without a solid concrete foundation beneath it.

Keeping our relationship with God first and our relationship with our family and friends second before our occupations are the sand, mortar and water our lives need to withstand the tests that time presents to us. To truly make it to the destination God has assigned to your life, you must have the proper priorities and have them ranked properly. None of us can make it to our destiny all by ourselves. We need the support of God, our families, and friends to truly be our best in the areas in which we were created to function in.

Chapter 16 Questions

1. What are my life priorities in order of importance to me?

_____

_____

_____

_____

2. Are my priorities in the proper order needed to fulfill my destiny?

_____

_____

_____

_____

3. Do I represent God daily both in public and in private?

_____

_____

_____

_____

4. Who are my true friends?

_____

_____

_____

_____

5. How well do I treat my family members and/or the individuals I consider to be my friends?

_____

_____

_____

_____

Chapter 17

We Are All Equal Pieces To The Puzzle

As a child I often sat in church on Sundays and wondered why people would cry during the service. Certain songs would be played or certain words would be spoken and people would cry. As I grew older I was finally able to understand why. The answer that I uncovered is that we never know what other people are going through or have gone through unless they reveal it to us.

As we go through our lives we will experience times of pain and times of trouble. We make it through difficult situations and know beyond a shadow of a doubt that it was God who brought us through it. Everyone has secrets, and each of us has things that we are ashamed to share with others. Take a look around you, there are people who look happy on the outside, but are sad and broken on the inside. It might even be the person who stares back at you in the mirror.

Everyone Is Important

All over this world people walk around with an uncaring and uncompassionate disposition for the plight of others. They attempt to avoid homeless people and others who they feel are living at a level beneath them. They watch the news and see stories of crime, job cuts and others suffering. It has no effect on them who view it with an uncaring attitude. Others walk around every day with the notion that if it does not happen in their neighborhood or to someone that they care about, they simply could care less. The truth is that none of us is above reproach. There is a much larger world out there than what exists within the confines of our living spaces. We have no clue who God will choose to place in our paths to enrich our lives.

Whatever a man sows he shall also reap. If we learn to bless others, the blessings will come back to us. Each person that we go out of our way to help represents a child of God. They are our brothers and sisters within him. In the book of Matthew chapter 25 verses 37-40 Jesus states, "Then shall the righteous answer him saying, Lord, when did we see you hungry and feed you, or thirsty and give you drink? When did we see you a stranger and take you in or naked and clothe you? Or when did we see you sick, or in prison, and come to you. And the King will answer and say to them, Assuredly, I say to you in as much as you did it to one of the least of these my brethren, you did it to me?"

Spirit Of Capitalism versus Christianity

In our walk with God we are tested every day to see if we are worthy of his divine promotion. A great number of people are missing out on their destiny because they are failing God's tests daily. The world teaches us that in order to succeed, we must be callous and cutthroat. God teaches us that we must be humble and kind to others in order to succeed. Which side are you going to choose?

It is a crying shame that in this world, profits are valued over the sanctity of human life. In the book of Matthew chapter 6 verse 24 Jesus states, "No one can serve two masters; for either he will hate the one and love the other, or else he will be loyal to the one and despise the other. You cannot serve God and mammon."

A lot of individuals feel the way to get ahead in this life is to undercut others, and claw their way to success. They worship at the altar of Capitalism and leave God and his

135

Kingdom principles in the dust. If you are one of those individuals I implore you to abandon this money-motivated method of thought. The truth is many of the same people that certain people scratch clawing their way to the top, will be the same ones that will be looking down at them after they fall. You never know who you are going to need in this life.

What I say here may not be popular in our capitalistic world, but it is the truth that I have observed from my vantage point. As I said earlier, companies do not care about you or your life situation. Their allegiance is to their shareholders. If you still do not believe me check out the story of a woman I met below.

Imagine working for a hospital for nearly 30 years and then finding out that you have a debilitating illness (multiple sclerosis) for which there is no cure. You are left physically and mentally unable to continue working due to the painful symptoms of your disease, and the side effects of the medications prescribed for you. No one understands the pain and suffering that you have to endure daily just to make it through life. To make matters worse, the hospital that you have given nearly 30 years of your life to has decided to challenge your claims for disability. They pursue this action against you despite the fact that their own doctors have diagnosed and treated you. You wonder to yourself, God what have I done to deserve this?

This is a real life example of what happens when the god of money leads us instead of the spirit of the true and living God. There is no excuse other than profit margin when a company that you have given your all to, will treat you as if they never knew you. This is not a Black, White, Latino or Asian story, it is an American reality. Companies like this would rather see their workers suffer rather than do the right thing for them. This type of heartless fiscally motivated behavior happens daily not just with hospitals, but also within the corporate world and with health care companies. It is a documented fact that the more claims that health insurance companies deny can lead to large monetary bonuses for their executives. It is a great injustice that people can sleep well at night knowing that their monetary greed leads directly to the suffering and death of others.

Unfortunately, there are many of us who have adopted the methods and ideologies of these corporations as we relate to other people. The wake up call does not come to us until the injustice affects the life of someone close to us. If this is your methodology it is never too late for you to start viewing others as individuals and not just numbers on a spreadsheet. This could be the very issue that is preventing God from unveiling your destiny to you.

To Those Wronged

To the people who may have been wronged, know that God knows your suffering and is always in your corner. For what others may question, God has all the answers. Let no one steal the joy or peace of mind that resonates within you. Let your love for God outweigh any anger and resentment for your employer or the insurance company. God still has his hand on you in spite of what you may have gone through, or are currently facing. Know that you could have been dead and gone, but the Lord's destiny for your life has kept you in the land of the living.

Your life is a testament to the greatness of God. Learn to let the resentment go and let God lead the way. You may say its too difficult, Eric you don't know what I have been through or are currently dealing with. The truth is I don't know, but our Father does. Please seek his voice and his advice. Take action only when he instructs you to do so. The instructions are revealed in your dreams, through your conscience, and in the warm positive feelings within your heart.

To The Decision Makers

If you happen to be in a decision making position learn to soften your heart instead of padding your wallet. Please understand that you could be a medical emergency away from bankruptcy court yourself. Know that no one chooses to be ill, but you can control how you respond to his or her illness. Put yourself in the shoes of the afflicted individual or that of their family. Once you do this, you will truly understand why love and compassion are better than money and profit margin. Stop treating people as if they were numbers on a balance sheet instead of children of God.

Having a heart may not give you a key to a new mansion, but it is an essential key to someday inhabiting the Kingdom of Heaven. In the book of Ezekiel chapter 36 verses 26-27 it states, "I will give you a new heart and put a new spirit within you; I will take the heart of stone out of your flesh and give you a heart of flesh. I will put my spirit within you and cause you to walk in my statues, and you will keep my judgments and do them."

Selfish to Selfless

America, there are too many people that live their lives possessing a heart of stone. Others may possess the heart of flesh, but the spirit of God is absent within it. A great number are choosing to live popularly instead of righteously. Countless people attend church Sunday after Sunday and raise hell in the world from Monday to Saturday. They treat others as if they are beneath them and wonder why the shores of their destiny escape the plane of their horizon. The selfish desires spawned from the fruit of capitalism are delaying and denying God's destiny for numerous people. When we seek the shores of selfishness, there will be plenty of money awaiting our arrival there. The problem will reveal itself when we realize that the favor of God and his presence will be absent from it.

This is the reason why drug dealers look over their shoulders and why some people from all walks of life ranging from corporate CEO's to ministers get greedy. For many of us these are the individuals that we see and mistake for inhabitants of destiny. Their true motivations manifest themselves in the fruit that their words and actions produce. There are legions of people in our world pillaging their own crops and bearing rotten fruit with their works. There are many of us who spend our lives eating the rotten fruit and wondering why it makes us sick instead of satisfying our hunger.

The Helper

As believers, God has equipped us with his Holy Spirit to discern for us where the rotten fruit lies to protect us from it. The Holy Spirit was sent to earth when Jesus ascended into Heaven in the days following his crucifixion. To acquire this layer of protection you must have a personal relationship with God. When you know God for yourself it qualifies you to receive his divine instructions via the Holy Spirit. In the book of John chapter 14 verse 26 Jesus states, "But the Helper, the Holy Spirit, whom the Father will send in My name, He will teach you all things, and bring to your remembrance all things that I said to you."

You must acknowledge the Holy Spirit and be receptive of its revelations for you. You must hold on to your faith and onto the Christ led principles that it teaches you. When you die and meet God, your Pastor will not be there, neither will your family members, friends, bosses or the CEO of your company. It will be God, you, and the resume of actions that you have crafted in your life which will represent you.

In the Apostle Paul's letter to the Romans chapter 14 verses 12 and 13 it states, "So then every one of us shall give accounts of himself to God. Let us not therefore judge one another anymore: but judge rather that no man put a stumbling block or cause to fall in our brother's way." My friends we were put on earth to love and help one another, not to make life difficult on others. There comes a point when following the pack must dissipate and the leader in you must emerge.

It is God's will for us to treat people well regardless of their age, race, socioeconomic background, religion or political affiliation. Our lives are being watched and only we have the power to control what God is seeing from us. When we do the best we can for our fellow man, we pass God's test with flying colors.

This life is a one shot audition to earn a position in the Kingdom of Heaven. There are millions of people who would rather follow the world's ideology into hell rather than God's into Heaven. Other than people who are about to be executed as a means of capital punishment, I know of no other individuals who have an advance notice of the hour of their death. None of us truly knows how much time we have on this earth. In a world where people are alive and healthy one day and deceased within the same day, we must strive to live a life that God is proud to direct.

When we enrich the lives of others, our lives are enriched. Let us leave the judging up to God, and try to help others instead of hurting them. Our change happens when we dedicate ourselves to doing it one day at a time. What we say and do today could possibly be the last words and actions that the world will know us for. Please make the decision to take none of God's given days for granted as well as none of his children. Just as every day is a gift, every person is a gift from God as well.

The Structure

In the sports world the mission of a team is to take a group and unite them under a common goal of winning a championship. An owner puts individuals on the team together with this vision in mind. In order for the team to win every player must contribute. Their contributions are measured by the statistics they accumulate. The job of the coaches is to motivate and bring out the best that the players have to give. Below I have listed the structure of a sports team.

Sports Team Structure

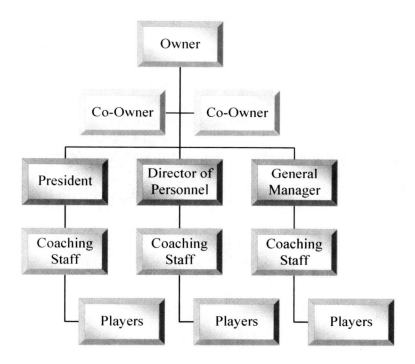

The Kingdom of God is very similar to the sports world. In God's kingdom his mission is to take his children and unite us under a common goal of making it to Heaven. We are all sent to earth with this vision in mind. In order for us to win we all must make contributions. Our contributions are measured by the lives we touch, and how well we use our God given gifts and talents.

In the Christian way of life, there is one principal owner and two co-owners. God is the principal owner, and Jesus

Christ and the Holy Spirit represent the co-ownership group. Jesus is also the Kingdom President, Director of Player Personnel and the General Manager.

The purpose of God's coaching staff (clergy) is to encourage us players (laymen and laywomen) and motivate us to bring out the best we have to give to the world. The members of the coaching staff serve as both players and coaches at the same time. They are players who have received and heeded God's call on their life to minister to other players.

They do not possess a more direct line to God, Jesus, and the Holy Spirit than the players who are not called to serve as clergy do. They are still normal men and women no matter what some individuals may claim. The players are made up of laymen and laywomen who have not been called by God to serve as clergy. The power of the Holy Spirit is sent by God to guide both the coaching staff and the players.

Kingdom of God Structure

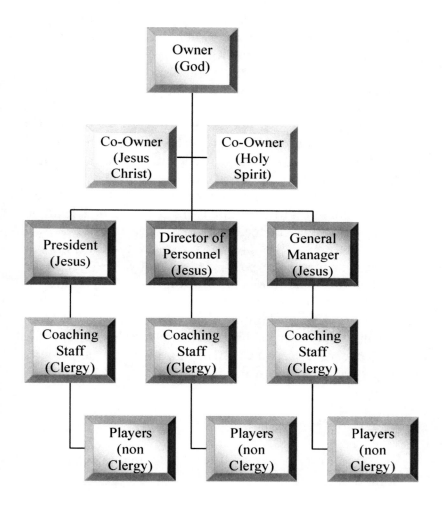

The Power Of The Holy Spirit

In the book of John chapter 14 verses 15-17 Jesus states, "If you love me keep my commandments. And I will pray the Father, and he will give you another Helper, that He may abide with you forever. The Spirit of truth, whom the world cannot receive, because it neither sees him nor knows him; but you know him, for he dwells with you and will be in you." This passage lets us know that the Holy Spirit resides in each of us if we choose to activate it. Its power is manifested through our actions.

The power of God's Holy Spirit allows each of us who receives it to fully function at the maximum capacity that God created us to do. In John chapter 14 verse 6 Jesus reveals himself as the intercessor between God and his children. He states, "I am the way, the truth and the life. No one comes to the father except through me." This is indicated on the kingdom chart shown on page 143.

We are all equal and integral pieces to the puzzle of God's kingdom. When we all work together and learn to position our pieces in their correct places, the puzzle will become spectacular. The pieces we seek are found within our purpose. Our pieces are positioned correctly when we make it our mission to do God's will for our lives. His will is for each of us to discover our purpose for being and live righteously within it daily at a place called destiny. We all have work to do to make this vision a reality. It should be the goal of everyone to someday earn an invite to the owner's skybox suite, better known as Heaven.

Chapter 17 Questions

1. Do I view every life as significant including my own?

_____

_____

_____

_____

2. Is the pull of capitalism more important to me than the call of God?

_____

_____

_____

_____

3. Is it better for me to live the popular way or the righteous way?

_____

_____

_____

_____

4. Do I understand the level of power that God's Holy Spirit can equip me with?

_____

_____

_____

_____

5. Is God's Holy Spirit activated within me?

_____

_____

_____

_____

PART FOUR

Thursday

CLOSING IN ON DESTINY

Chapter 18

Transforming Hopelessness Into Hope & Hope Into Action

The foundation for any dreams we may have in this life is hope. Whenever we feel that we have nowhere else to turn, it is hope that beckons us to cling to it. Hope provides us with a reason to get out of bed each day to face whatever the world sends our way. Webster's dictionary defines hope as a feeling that what is wanted will happen; desire accompanied by expectation.

Hope takes on several different forms to different individuals. Some people have abandoned hope, some have allowed it to be taken from them, some simply cling to it, and others transform it into action. For each of us to reach our destiny and live as functioning actors, hope must be transformed into action.

The first step is determining exactly what it is we are hoping for in the first place. For our hope to eventually become a reality there must be a vision of what our destination will look like when we arrive. We must acknowledge the calling on our life, make a plan to reach it and then begin the journey to it. This chapter may save someone's life or help someone else transition from simply hoping to finally acting on their hope in pursuit of their destiny.

Words To The Hopeless

There is someone reading this right now feeling that your life is hopeless. You have abandoned your hope. You have been suffering with the effects of physical, emotional or spiritual pain. In your life you may feel that giving up on life or your dreams is the only escape route from the situation you are facing. You are suffering in silence crying yourself to sleep every night not caring if you awake the next day. You have heard about God and Jesus your whole life, but you feel they have no time for you.

People have hurt you and the world has been beating you up for a long time. You feel a feeling of shame with the thought of sharing your innermost feelings with someone else. For many years the pain of physical, sexual and/or emotional trauma has robbed you of your ability to feel like a complete person. Being wronged is something only the person wronged and God can understand. Know that through him resides the victory over your feelings of victimization.

For others it may be a sudden loss of a loved one, a job loss or a lack of life fulfillment that has you teetering on the edge of life. You may feel that if you died that no one would miss you and if they did they would soon get over it. In your mind you feel that the predicament you are seemingly stuck in features no escape route for you. I implore you to refrain from quitting on life or your dreams.

The key to escaping your predicament is taking the time to tailor your focus on finding solutions instead of fretting over your problems. Know that God has a solution for every situation. Your destiny could be just beyond your scope of vision. God loves you and I love you if you feel that no one else does. The purpose that he has for your life is real. You may feel misunderstood by people, but know that God understands everything. Take a look back over your life and reflect on how many dire circumstances that God has brought you through. Know that if God was finished with you, your life would have ended long ago.

You must muster the resolve to rekindle your faith. Our faith serves as the flotation mechanism for our hope. Through all the despair, disappointment and depression you are still standing. God did not bring you this far to leave you desolate and dreamless. Every life is a gift from God, including yours. Leave the negative thoughts to be what they are which is simply negative thoughts. The key is to not allow those negative thoughts to become negative actions.

Hopelessness is the chief promoter of poor decisions. God did not see fit to place us on this earth for us to live without aspirations. Anything worthy of accomplishment must first be aspired to. It is the destiny of no one to become a life victim. It is God's plan for each of his children to be victorious instead. Just look back over your life and you will find someone who has loved and cared about you.

There is no way to make it to adulthood without at least one person loving you along the way. There was someone who made sure that you were taken care of at some point. Just take a look at yourself now; you may not be everything that you would like to be, but its okay. The sun will rise again tomorrow and it will bring you another opportunity to press the reset button on your life.

Every day above ground represents new opportunities and possibilities for your life. Your life has just been plugged into the wrong outlet. Plug it into another one labeled hope and let God recharge your life and your dreams. Please use the space below in the left column to write 10 things or people that are worth getting up every day for. In the right column write 10 things that make your life not worth getting up for every day.

Worth It	Not Worth It

Even if you listed more things in the not worth it column, here is a fact. The love of God and his designed purpose for your life outweighs any potential reasons why you may feel that life is not worth getting up daily for. You could feel trapped in the land of security, or in the midst of transitioning to your destiny, but no matter where you are never let hopelessness force you to quit on life or the dreams that God placed in you. As long as air is being drawn in and out of your lungs, the opportunity for positive change awaits you. In the book of Psalms chapter 55 verse 22 it states, "Cast your burden on the Lord, and he shall sustain you; He shall never permit the righteous to be moved."

This means that when you feel the weight of the world on your shoulders give it to God. Go to him in prayer tell him about your troubles, and he has the power to make a way out of no way. He will never allow the righteous to fail, just trust in him. Remember that disappointment, despair and depression are not your masters. Do not obey the prescriptions they have been recommending for your life. God is your master and failing has never been his claim to fame. God, Jesus Christ, and Eric Moore all love you and nothing will change that fact. In your point of hopelessness give hope to someone else and watch the power of God come alive within you. Remember to also keep your head held high, because the beauty of Heaven cannot be seen if your vision is trained downward.

Hope Taken

The second group of individuals has allowed their hope to be taken away. Those afflicted by this condition have allowed dream thieves and critics to steal their hope. The critics say things such as you don't have what it takes, you are too young or old, you are not educated enough, you don't have a specific look or have the right connections to make your dreams a reality. Many people unfortunately have allowed the opinion that someone imposes on them to become their personal reality. So many of us get caught up doing what other people think we should do with our lives that we fail to seek God's plan.

To be frank many of us are cowards who let other cowards steal our dreams. We craft lives and surround ourselves with fear and mediocrity as our best friends. Please realize that no one has a greater stake in your success than you do. You must learn to stand up for yourself in this life and never get tired enough to sit down. Scores of people have been sitting for so long that they have forgotten what it feels like to stand.

In the 1939 film The Wizard of Oz, the cowardly lion only had one wish to be granted whenever he met the wizard. His one wish was to be granted the gift of courage. When he finally met the wizard, the wizard gave him a medal with the word courage displayed on it. The lion then realized that he truly had nothing to fear. With the wizard's help, the lion realized that the courage he sought was self contained.

Our world is filled with cowardly lions that go through their lives never realizing that the courage they seek is found within them already. The hallmarks of a lion are their courage and strength. Life should not be lived in a cowardly fashion but courageously and boldly instead. Life is too short to go through it afraid of maximizing your potential and lived hopelessly.

Having hope is a choice that you should never allow another person to steal from you. It is hope that keeps us pushing forward when goals seem unattainable. For many people our dreams are like New Years resolutions, we all have them but few of us follow through with them. It may seem intimidating or like your dreams may be difficult to attain, but you have to keep moving forward. When you push forward you make it incredibly difficult for someone else to push you backward.

Each of us must learn to be comfortable in our own self and acquire the gift of courage. Anything that has ever proven to be successful was originally birthed from the dream of someone. Hope is what allows us to believe that there is a better reality in the future for us than that which we are currently facing. Hope is what grants us the ability to believe that Heaven is real and that it is our reward for living lives pleasing to God.

A life without hope is a life without vision and a life without vision is as stable as a kite in the midst of a hurricane. The time has come to get your hope back and begin to visualize what your future can be starting today. Someone can only steal your hope if you allow him or her to. Create a security plan of prayer, positivity and courage. When this is done your hope will be safer than the gold locked away in Fort Knox. It is my sincere hope that you keep your hope alive.

Converting Hope Into Action

The third group of individuals have hope, but have held on to it for so long that it has created calluses on their dreams. They have thus far failed to convert their hope into action. They hear speech after speech, read book after book and witness God working in the lives of others. They are perplexed because it seems that their life has remained stationary and lacked growth. Year after year passes and they are in the same situation. Still they take their hope and hold on to it believing that someday things will change in their favor. The time for change is now.

For many of us our frustration grows and we drag through life unsure of how to improve our situations. We have permitted fear, negative past experiences of ourselves or others, and the lack of a ravenous hunger for change tether us to hope.

Possessing hope but neglecting to transform it into action is akin to waiting in front of an elevator, but never pressing the up or down button to take us anywhere. Countless numbers of us depend on God or someone else to press the button for us instead of making the decision to do it ourselves. The breakthrough for a person in this situation comes when their level of life discomfort becomes so great that it forces them to make a move. A fire must be lit under them.

There must come a point when the message sinks in to us that we have gifts and talents that are eroding within us. We take a look around at the majority of people around us in the same situation and all everyone talks about is what they hope to do. We sit around and expect God to give us his maximum while we give the minimum.

In order to make it to your destiny, your hope must become a written plan and that plan must be implemented. Anticipation must become application. There must be a fundamental change in your mentality. You will only be as successful as your mind will allow you to believe you can be. We all dream of reaching our dreams, but most of us never snap out of the dream to create the plan to dream living.

If we fail to advance beyond the hope stage, our destiny will never be fulfilled. The role of hope is to get us through the tough times, but our plans and the actions that succeed them pave the way for us to make it to the great times. Most individuals who never advance beyond hope are clueless in terms of God's purpose for their lives. Many of them do not even consider it.

Think about it, why would God grant us life here on earth to spend it hoping the whole time for a better one? The truth is he sent us here equipped with jackhammers of gifts and anvils of talents to breakthrough hope and carry out our assignments tailor made for us.

When we hold on to hope and neglect to act on it, our calling is suppressed. This is the reason why millions of people live frustrated and unfulfilled lives. The true calling of your life is revealed when God's instruction, your passion, and your gifts and talents unite.

Why are you laying in bed every Sunday night hoping Monday through Thursday will disappear and magically become Friday? The reason it becomes harder and harder to get out of bed is because your gifts and talents are not being used properly daily. You settled for a job to pay bills instead of seeking a destiny to fulfill your calling.

Take the time today and write down exactly what it is that you are passionate about. What is it that you would do for free, but will allow you to be compensated to your satisfaction? Don't worry about what other people may say or think about your idea. This is your life and these are the dreams that God has placed in your heart. You have held them as your personal prisoners of hope. The time has come to set them free.

There is someone reading this right now who knows the nine to five way of life is not for them. Starting your own business may be your dream. For someone else it may be advancing at your current job or finding one that fits your strengths. Someone else reading this may be feeling trapped in the clutches of an unfruitful life. What are you hoping for?

All of these situations have the potential to be overcome in your favor. Do not be afraid to take action when you know that God has put the calling in you. Before you take action physically, the first step is to create your plan mentally. Today brainstorm and write down ideas on where and how your dream will thrive. Then write down systematic goals for attaining what it is that you seek. Create your goals in realistic step-by-step increments. Once your first goal list has been achieved create a new list of goals.

Remember to separate your goals by short term (within one year) and long term (more than one year). Pray over them and ask God for the power of his anointing to saturate your goals. Try to dedicate at least five hours per week solely dedicated to perfecting your craft. Your breakthrough may be six months or six years away, but if you put in the sweat equity you will be ready whenever God's will permits it to be fulfilled.

To go anywhere worth reaching, you must write down where you are going and your plans for making it there. If planning and action do not follow hope, nothing will ever change for you. Ninety percent of success is planning to be there and executing that plan. People all over the world pray for God to move in their lives, but they neglect to define specifically where or how they desire his movement. The book of Habakkuk chapter 2 versus 1-2 states, "I will stand upon my watch, and set me upon the tower, and will watch to see what he will say unto me, and what shall I answer when I am reproved. And the Lord answered me and said, write the vision and make it plain upon tablets, that he may run that reads it."

This passage lets us know that our vision must be written down. When we write down our vision and goals, they serve as daily reminders of where we are going in our lives. It becomes the written directions for our journey. You can start that business, seek training, go back to school and improve your life situation. Allow your passion to lead you into preparation, which will place you on the pathway to your destiny.

Chapter 18 Questions

1. What will it take for me to transform my hopelessness into hope?

_____

_____

_____

_____

2. What steps do I need to take to transform my hope into action?

_____

_____

_____

_____

3. What are my goals for the next 365 days in terms of improving my quality of life?

_____

_____

_____

_____

4. What are my goals for the next 5 years?

_____

_____

_____

_____

5. Where do I see myself in 10 years?

_____

_____

_____

_____

Chapter 19

God's Timing Is Always Better Than Yours

None of us living had the power to determine the following: Who we were born to? What purpose we were born to fulfill? When we were born? Where we were born? How we would we be raised, and why we were born in the era we were? Over the course of our lives we fill in the myriad of questions with answers. It is up to us to determine who we really are on this earth, what purpose God sent us here to fulfill, when we will put our life in God's hands, where our lives will have the most impact, how we will best use our God given gifts and talents, and why God felt we would be at our best within the era that we live in.

In the book of Acts chapter 17 verses 26-27 the Apostle Paul helps us reinforce our answers. He wrote, "And he has made from one blood every nation of men to dwell on all the face of the earth, and has determined their pre-appointed times and the boundaries of their dwellings, so that they should seek the Lord, in the hope that they might grope for Him and find Him, though He is not far from each one of us." With his infinite wisdom God knew exactly where and when to send us to fulfill the mission he has for us.

Perfectly Timed

Imagine if basketball legend Michael Jordan was born in 1863 instead of 1963. Would there have been a game called basketball for him to revolutionize? Imagine if computer maven Bill Gates was born in 1855 instead of 1955. Would there have been a computer industry for him to effectively innovate? Then imagine if inventor Thomas Edison was born in 1947 instead of 1847. Would there have been electrical innovations for him to implement? Finally imagine if Ford Motor Company founder Henry Ford was born in 1963 instead of 1863. Would there have been vehicle assembly lines for him to pioneer?

Each of these individuals was born at a time when the tools that God gave them could be maximized. God knew exactly when the world would be able to receive the best benefits from their gifts and talents. We may not have pioneered assembly lines or turned Nike, Microsoft, Edison and Ford into household names; however there is still the ability for greatness in each of us. When God sent us to earth, he knew exactly when to send us, where to send us, and which family to send us to. The environments and cultures in which we allow ourselves to be immersed foster the growth of our abilities.

There are prime tasks for all of us to complete within the era in which we all live. We were not born fifty or one hundred years before or after the date God ordered for our lives. He knew exactly when the world would need the gifts and talents that he placed in us. God knows exactly who to use, and precisely what tasks to use them for.

My Life

In my own life I have learned that the timing of God works in our best interest. If it were up to me, this book would have been written in 2004. Back then I felt that the timing was right and that I was ready to challenge the world with my pen. The problem was when I would try to write, the words seemed inauthentic. The truth is, at that point in my life; I really hadn't lived or closely witnessed many of the situations that I've elaborated on in this book. My work at that time looked as if it would have been guesswork and not genuine.

There are many of you reading this that have battled the circumstances of the world longer than I have been alive. The thing is I have been able to take my lessons learned, and those of individuals who have inhabited the earth longer than I and make them relatable to everyone who reads it within these pages. Over the past several years, I have done something that most people never do. I have found my voice in this world.

The inconvenient truth is that most people never find their voice in this world. Scores of people have allowed their voices to be silenced or drowned out by others. I have learned that unless you find your voice in this world, someone else will speak for you.

Just as importantly as finding my voice, I had to learn the proper time to let my voice be heard. Several years ago I knew the goodness of God, but I lacked the knowledge of his greatness. I had to go through some difficult circumstances and had to experience the power of God moving within my own life firsthand.

Looking back now I realize that God allows us to go through difficult circumstances and then he decides to pull us out just in time. I refer to these times as spiritual credit checks. They are evaluators of our faith scores and let us know that God is the only one who deserves the credit for our deliverance. Through it all, I had to grow into the person who wrote this book.

For the past several years I wrote fiction, but I didn't have a passion for the work I was producing. During that same time period, unbeknownst to me, I had been accumulating research materials for this book. God knew better than I that this book would be best received in 2012 and beyond as opposed to 2004.

Back then an economic calamity was an unimaginable concept in the United States of America. For most people their lives had been business as usual up until that point. So much has happened in our country since then, where normal life has gone from people skating by, to people scraping just to get buy.

In 2004, I had all the tools to make a good book, but I lacked the seasoning to make a great one. Many times when we feel we are ready to do something, for some reason or another our timing turns out being inaccurate. This is simply because we have proceeded with our timetable instead of God's. Our time of seasoning allows us the time to transition from goodness to greatness. For some of us goodness or mediocrity is good enough in our minds. The problem with this mentality is it robs us of the ability to operate fully at the level that we were designed to.

In the book of Malachi chapter 3 verse 8 it states, "Will a man rob God? Yet you have robbed me! But you say, In what way have we robbed you? In tithes and offerings." The lack of tithes and offerings is not the only way we can rob God. When we neglect to figure out our purpose and fully implement our gifts and talents, we rob God of his investment in us. Many people hold him hostage nightly praying for the ransom of abilities and tools that he has already placed within them. The period of seasoning allows us time to develop and toughen up to properly handle the rigors of operating in greatness. Times of seasoning are not easy but are nonetheless critical seasons that force us to trust in God's timing.

President Barack Obama

Take a look at the life of our current President Barack Obama. After his July 2004 address at the Democratic National Convention, many observers felt that he should have been seeking the nomination Presidential nomination of his party instead of Senator John Kerry. The main issues preventing this were, he was not ready to run for President, and the country at the time was not ready to elect a biracial, two term state Senator from Illinois. After four years of seasoning in the United States Senate, Barack Obama was ready to run for President in 2008.

All the mannerisms and character traits he possessed in 2008 were present in 2004, but back then he simply was not ready to run. Who knows, if he had possibly run for President in 2004 he may have made a good Presidential candidate then. The thing is, both he and God knew that 4 years as a US Senator would prepare him for potential greatness in 2008. The reason that he was able to win the presidential election in 2008 was due to the change in this country's social, economic and political climates from 2004-2008.

He didn't neglect his time of seasoning, and in 2008 it paid off in the form of a Presidential victory that for centuries seemed impossible. Many of us have fought or neglected our times of seasoning. This has caused a great number of us to sacrifice greatness for goodness and mediocrity instead. Seasoning allows us to find our voices and truly project them onto the landscape of life at the correct time. You may agree or disagree with his political views, but the story of his four-year rise to his destiny is an inspiration to millions.

Joel Osteen

If the example of President Obama does not do it for you, take a look at the life of Joel Osteen. For 17 years he worked faithfully behind the scenes in his father John's ministry. In 1999, his father passed away and Joel assumed leadership of his dad's church. To the surprise of many including him, over the past 13 years he has taken the church his father built and made its ministry flourish. Imagine if his father would have passed away in 1979 or 1989, would Joel have been ready to lead? In those 17 years from 1982-1999 he acquired the seasoning that was required to fulfill his destiny. He had no clue what God had waiting for him around the corner. Since 1999, he has sold millions of books and inspired a nation of people to live their best lives now. He could have easily grumbled and not given his best over those 17 years, and simultaneously blew God's plans for promoting him.

Like Joel and Barack each one of us must learn to be great soldiers before God sees fit to promote us to become great leaders. There are some people reading this who desire to own a business, but have never mastered the art of becoming a great employee first. When you work hard and are diligent in areas that lack your passion, God sees you. Your work contributes to the equity of your destiny.

God saw what Joel and Barack were doing in the mean time, and saw fit to promote them when he knew they were ready. Some of us may feel we are ready for our destiny, and others of us may feel that we are not ready. No matter which way we feel, it is God who ultimately decides when the timing is right for us. It is our responsibility to prepare for it.

You may or may not agree with their messages, but President Obama and Pastor Osteen have inspired millions of people to uncover their own greatness. Would they have been just as successful in 1998 or 2018 as opposed to 2008? Quite frankly it does not matter. God knew the exact time when they would be properly seasoned for greatness.

Seasoning and Refinement

Have you ever tried to eat a piece of chicken or steak raw? I hope not, but if you did, you most likely would have been a victim of salmonella or E coli poisoning respectively. Both meats must be cooked to have the possibility to both taste good and provide nutritional value. To truly reach their full taste potential, the meats must be seasoned during their preparation.

Our lives are similar to the meats. Theoretically we may feel that we are ready to be what God created us to be due to our combination of gifts, talents and life experiences. The thing is, the master chef (God), only knows when we have been fully cooked and ready to serve. The refinement of and shaping of our gifts and talents represent the cooking process, but our lessons gleaned from our life experiences represent the seasoning that prepares us for greatness.

Legions of individuals have allowed their lives to be microwaved instead of grilled, baked and broiled. We are the products of a society that demands right now results for things that take quality time to create. The problem with the microwave process is it renders the seasoning ineffective because it does not allow it the proper timing to marinate into our lives. The microwave process would have allowed us to appear to be well done on the outside sooner, but as soon as the blades of life cut into us we would hemorrhage.

God knows the cooking process allows both our outside and inside to be cooked evenly. Impatience with the timing of God has caused scores of people to contaminate and poison their destiny. You must learn to trust in the timing of God. He knows when you are properly seasoned, fully cooked and ready to serve the world with what he placed within you.

If this book had been written in 2004 or if Joel Osteen became Pastor in 1989 and Barack Obama President in 2004, things potentially would not have worked in our best interest. In my case, the world would not have been receptive to a book about life improvement from a young man with limited life experience. Another reason it would not have been appreciated is at that time, most people were not concerned with searching for the greater meaning of their lives.

The fundamental collective mind shift did not happen until the US recession spawned streams of personal great depressions in the lives of millions of hard working Americans. If Barack Obama would have become President in 2004, he would have presided over two wars and the largest economic collapse since the Great Depression. He likely would have lost a re-election bid in 2008, and would have missed out on his critical period of seasoning as a United States Senator. If Joel Osteen would have become Pastor of Lakewood church in 1989, he would have been a

26-year-old unknown Pastor from Houston, Texas. At that time he would have lacked the mediums of cable television and the Internet to reach his full effectiveness.

These samples above are all examples of the ways in which God can protect us from unnecessary failure. God sets up both the situation and the space for our abilities to thrive within them without our knowledge. Many times when we feel that God is doing nothing, he is simply safe guarding and preparing our future beyond our field of vision. The timing of God provides us with layers of insulation and protection from things we cannot see.

Imagine if Jesus had come to earth one hundred years before or one hundred years after he actually did. Would there have been twelve disciples ready and willing to follow him? Would St. Peter and the Apostle Paul have been able to spearhead the Christian movement?

God knew exactly when Jesus needed to be sent to earth, where to send him to and exactly who would take his message to the next level. God sent Jesus to earth at the exact point when he felt that the gifts and talents placed in him would be maximized. In the three years that Jesus preached his message, the information he imparted is still valid nearly 2,000 years later.

The timing of God could have very well saved you from an automobile accident last night or this morning. How many times have you taken your normal route a little late to your destination and discovered accidents where you would have been had you been on time? Or how many times have you taken your normal route a little early and later discovered that a bad accident happened on your route at the normal time you would have been there. We never know the danger God's timing may be shielding us from.

Each one of the individuals I listed in this chapter had greatness in them, but it had to be manifested at the right time. The time period of refinement of our gifts and talents mixed in with our life experiences is an invaluable resource. There are many of us that neglect our time of refinement and end up paying a steep price for it.

There is a time and a place for everything and your arrival at your destiny is not extraneous from that fact. There is nothing worse than being presented with the opportunity of a lifetime and being unprepared for it. When you do your part and prepare for greatness, God will take care of the timing.

You may not be a writer, a minister or even a politician, but the timing of God that has benefited each of us is working in your life at this moment. Know that the timing of God is always in your best interest. Always aim to be at your best in whatever you do, because you never know when the timing of God will change your life to.

Chapter 19 Questions

1. Have I learned to trust in the timing of God?

_____

_____

_____

_____

2. Am I properly seasoned and ready to serve in the capacity that God created me for?

_____

_____

_____

_____

3. Am I robbing God of his investment within me or am I paying him dividends through my work on earth?

_____

_____

_____

_____

4. Has my impatience with God's timing delayed or denied my destiny up until this point?

_____

_____

_____

_____

Chapter 20

Your Start Does Not Determine Your Finish

People worldwide have used their circumstances as an excuse for why they are destined to live their lives far below their potential. The time for this way of thinking has passed. The gifts and talents that God placed within us when used properly will elevate us to heights beyond the spectrum of our dreams. You do not have to know someone personally to be inspired by their story.

Each person that lives on this earth has a story to tell. As I said earlier, God has given us the tools that we need to create beautiful masterpieces with our lives. Your masterpiece is the portrait of your life in which the world is able to see the reflection of God's work through you. They are designed on canvases, which represent either the circumstances you were born into or the circumstances that you encounter on your journey through life. Its wrinkles and stains represent the adversity you face.

For some individuals the canvas they were initially given by God may have been presented to them wrinkled or stained. They may not have been given a pristine white surface to design their lives on. However, this does not matter since God made sure that each one of us was given the highest quality tools (gifts and talents) to design our canvases with.

There are scores of people that have let their wrinkled or stained canvases prevent them from designing their lives to the best of their abilities. They have convinced themselves that the problems with their canvases are unable to be painted over by the high quality tools that God has placed in them. Others refuse to paint or all together stop designing on their canvas due to the feeling that their prior or current life circumstances disqualify them from greatness. They forget that no matter what their given canvas looks like; God has supplied the tools they need to design their destiny right over it.

In the book of Isaiah chapter 43 verses 18-19 it states, "Do not remember the former things, nor consider the things of old. Behold, I will do a new thing, now it shall spring forth; Shall you not know it? I will even make a road in the wilderness and rivers in the desert." Our God is a restoration specialist, especially when it comes to dreams. The key is to still design your masterpiece despite the condition of the canvas that you have.

There are many of us who master our craft so well that our designs turn out head and shoulders above those who began life with a pristine white surface to design on. No matter how your life began or has gone, it does not ultimately determine your destiny. Each of us possesses the power to design our lives on the canvas that God blessed us with. In this chapter, I will give you examples of people who have achieved greatness with their tools despite the condition of their canvas. Each of them has created a personal masterpiece of true American inspiration.

Greg Mathis

He began his life in the Herman Gardens housing projects, one of the most dangerous and notorious places in the city of Detroit, Michigan. There were gangs, drug dealers, pimps and prostitutes all around him. Growing up the fourth child of a single mother, Greg Mathis eventually became a gang member hanging tough with the city's notorious Errol Flynn gang. At age 17, Mathis was arrested and served time in the county jail.

While in jail his mother broke the news to him that she had been diagnosed with terminal cancer. This news was the motivation he needed to commit to turning his life around. He realized that God did not create him to represent an inmate number in a prison, or a premature burial plot in a cemetery. As a promise to his mother, he decided to go back to school and abandon his previous life of crime. Mathis was subsequently able to get into college, and eventually law school with the expungement of his previous criminal record.

By 1995, he was elected as a Superior Court Judge in the State of Michigan. Since then he has eventually gone on to write his own autobiographical account titled Inner City Miracle, and as of this writing is currently starring in his own syndicated television show. With the assistance of God, he has transformed his life from being an antagonist of the law, to becoming an administrator of it. He refused to allow his inauspicious beginnings to deny him from the destiny that God created for him to fulfill.

At some point people may have written him off as a person with a one-way express ticket to prison or a cemetery. Judge Greg Mathis mustered the courage to turn his once disappointing life, into the awe inspiring discovery of his divine destiny. Once he changed his mental focus, a world filled with opportunities opened up for him. With his effort and God's favor, he turned his wrinkled and stained canvas into a legal masterpiece.

Oprah Winfrey

Her life began immersed in the poverty stricken Mississippi Delta in 1954. Up until age six, her loving and supportive grandmother raised her. Her grandmother also gave her the foundation for her future love of education, by encouraging her to read and recite Bible verses. At age six she was sent to live with her mother in Milwaukee, Wisconsin. Over the next eight years she would deal with a dysfunctional family life, which saw her sexually abused repeatedly by relatives who should have been protecting her.

Through it all she poured herself into her schoolwork, and was eventually sent to live with her father in Tennessee. There her gifts revealed themselves in the form of her superior communication skills. Oprah Winfrey eventually earned a full scholarship to Tennessee State University majoring in communications. After graduating she became a TV news anchor in Nashville, Tennessee and eventually in Baltimore, Maryland.

In 1983, Winfrey moved to Chicago, Illinois to host a local TV morning show called AM Chicago. It soon became the highest rated talk show in the city of Chicago. By 1986, AM Chicago became the nationally syndicated Oprah Winfrey Show, which has since then gone on to arguably become the most successful talk show in television history.

As of 2012, Oprah Winfrey through her production company Harpo has gone on to produce successful daytime talk shows for Dr. Phillip McGraw and Chef Rachael Ray. She has also branched off into producing the highly successful O magazine, established her own Satellite Radio Channel and managed to launch her OWN network in 2011.

Through all the tough times and negative situations Oprah held on to God's hand, and used the gifts and talents he gave her to touch and inspire the world. Oprah has risen from the sour predicament of poverty, to the sweet pinnacle of prestige. Some may have felt she was destined for a life of disappointment, but God made sure that her destiny of success would not be denied.

Her canvas was wrinkled and stained, but through sheer grit, determination and God's grace she turned it into a media masterpiece. Many people consider her to be the most powerful woman in the world, but even she knows that without the guidance of God she would be powerless. The life of Oprah Winfrey is glistening proof that a touch of God's favor can transform any life from the outhouse of oppression to the penthouse of promise. The early part of her life may have started out on the rough side of the mountain, but now she can pay cash for and own any mountain her heart desires to.

Marshall Mathers

The life of Marshall Mathers began in Missouri, where his single mother raised him bouncing from town to town in that state. They eventually moved to Warren, Michigan, a blue-collar industrial suburb of Detroit. Growing up he dealt with poverty, school bullies, and a mother who feigned Munchausen Syndrome toward him. A condition in which his mother in her mind created symptoms of illness within him that did not exist. He also had to deal with his mother's alleged abuse of prescription medications and a lack of support for his dreams.

At age fourteen Mathers discovered an affinity for rap music. He didn't care much for school, and wound up repeating the ninth grade three times before finally dropping out for good at age seventeen. To many it seemed as if his life was destined to be mired in the muck of desolation and despair. He found that rapping over hip-hop beats was a way to express his feelings with the world.

For several years, he worked various odd jobs and continued to perfect his rap skills. He performed under the stage M&M, which were the initials for his first and last name. After the birth of his daughter Hailie in 1995, he dedicated himself to working harder to become a successful rapper.

The first step was changing the spelling of his stage name from M&M to the currently well-known spelling Eminem. Even though he was a young, unknown, Caucasian rapper from Detroit, he believed his dreams would come true. There was no blueprint for him to follow, but he was determined to blaze his own trail. To support his family, Mathers worked in a restaurant and sold copies of his independently recorded music to anyone who would purchase it. By 1997, his fortune was changing.

Early that year, he went to Los Angeles and competed in the Rap Olympics, which was a freestyle rap battling competition. Mathers wound up taking second place, but an Interscope Records intern took in his performance and was impressed. The intern subsequently obtained a demo tape from Mathers, and passed it on to Interscope Records President Jimmy Iovine. Iovine secured the demo tape from the intern and passed it onto legendary music producer Dr. Dre. Impressed with what he heard, Dr. Dre signed Mathers to his record label Aftermath Entertainment and platinum success soon followed.

In early 1998, Marshall Mathers was simply a twenty five year old high school dropout working in a restaurant to support his family. He was also a man with the ability to take words and rhythmically bring them to life over rap beats in an exceptional way. Mathers knew that the ticket to his true destiny was through sharing with the world, the music that resided in him. Through all the years of poverty, family conflict and lack of acceptance, Mathers still persevered to reach God's destiny for him. By the end of 1999, he was triple platinum selling international rap superstar and a music industry icon. His once wrinkled and stained canvas has become a platinum masterpiece of rhythmic greatness.

Chris Gardner

Gardner Rich and company is considered to be a successful stock brokerage firm based in Chicago, Illinois. Its founder Chris Gardner's pathway to destiny was paved on a road on which none of us desire the displeasure of having to travel on. In 1981, he was working as a medical supply salesman in San Francisco, California. The twenty- seven year old Gardner had just become a father for the first time, and was in a period of life evaluation. He realized that his meager yearly salary and unfulfilling work life were not what was best for his life.

One day while working his sales job, he spotted a red Ferrari and was intrigued by it. He located the owner of the vehicle, and asked him what he did for a living. The owner informed Gardner that he was a stockbroker. Even though he had no previous training as a stockbroker, Gardner instantly became determined to learn the trade and become successful at it.

Through the connections of the Ferrari driving stockbroker and armed with a dogged level of persistence, Gardner was able to secure a position within the Dean Witter stockbroker training program in 1982. He quit his medical equipment sales job to live on a $1,000 dollar a month training stipend.

During his time in the Dean Witter Program, his personal life crumbled around him. His live in girlfriend left him, and placed their son under his care for him to raise alone. To make matters worse, the rooming house he lived in did not accept children. The $1,000 dollars per month he earned in the training program simply was not enough income to afford Gardner and his son the opportunity to live in a suitable residence. As a result, Gardner joined the ranks of the homeless living in the rough and tumble Tenderloin District in San Francisco. Over the next year, Gardner and his son would call shelters, churches and even the restroom of a Bay Area Rapid Transit station home. Through it all, Gardner held on to hope, and showed up to the training program daily determined to be the best at his craft.

By 1983, after his year of personal hell and turmoil, things began to look up for Gardner. His hard work paid dividends in the form of a broker position at Bear Stearns & Company, and an apartment in the Bay Area near San Francisco. His life of living on the streets was over. From 1983-1987, Gardner worked as a broker at Bear Stearns and became a top earner during that time. After learning all that he could about the industry, Gardner opened his own brokerage firm in 1987. He named it Gardner Rich and relocated to Chicago, Illinois. Over the next fifteen years his company would grow into one of the top stock brokerage firms in the United States of America.

In 2002, his story was chronicled on the ABC network news show 20/20. His life story garnered a large amount of interest from Hollywood film producers. Four years later in 2006, Gardner's autobiography, The Pursuit of Happyness, and a feature film based on his life with the same name were released. The book became a New York Times bestseller, and the film starring Will Smith, went on to gross more than 300 million dollars at the box office.

Chris Gardner has gone from the pit of homelessness, to a prime residence located in the center of God's destiny for his life. His story has inspired everyone that hears it to keep dreaming even if his or her current life is a ghastly nightmare. Even in his condition of homelessness, his faith in God never permitted him to be hopeless. His once wrinkled and stained canvas has become a life portfolio stocked and bonded with blue chip inspiration and exponential achievement.

Bernard Hopkins

In the world of boxing many consider him to be the greatest counter puncher who has ever lived. For Bernard Hopkins, the art of counter punching has not just been his signature style in the ring, but the method in which he has battled life. As a young adolescent, Hopkins early battles were primarily with law and order, the undisputed heavyweight champions of the criminal justice system.

By age eighteen he had been arrested over thirty times, and was driving his life on the road to perdition steering with both hands. His mother did the best that she could for him by moving their family from the notorious Raymond Rosen projects in Philadelphia, Pennsylvania, to a better neighborhood within the Germantown section of the city. The move did less to help Hopkins as much as it pushed him deeper into the allure of the streets. He developed a reputation and a rap sheet that featured assault and robbery as his criminal calling cards.

By 1983, at age eighteen, the long arm of the law finally grasped Bernard Hopkins within its clutches. He was sent upstate to Graterford State Prison on an eighteen- year sentence as a consequence for multiple felonies. It was at Graterford where he realized that he wasn't the toughest man on the planet, let alone in the state of Pennsylvania.

Looking for an opportunity to do his time more constructively, Hopkins became enamored with the inmate boxing program run inside Graterford. In 1984, he joined the program and his ability as a fighter began to manifest itself. With the aide of inmate trainer Michael "Smokey" Wilson, Hopkins became a boxing legend within the confines of the prison's walls. Wilson believed in his abilities as a fighter and spoke life into him by proclaiming that one day Hopkins would be the middleweight champion of the world. In boxing, Hopkins discovered his calling and began to treat every day as an opportunity to master his craft.

Five years into his eighteen-year sentence, Hopkins was released from prison in 1988. The twenty-three year old Hopkins was determined to never go back to prison, and maximize his abilities as a boxer. In October of that year he turned professional. He lost his debut fight, but was determined to deter the setback from denying his destiny. The loss made him work harder, and helped serve as a catalyst to renew his focus. He teamed up with trainer Bouie Fisher and over the next seven years built up an impressive fighting resume.

In April of 1995, Hopkins defeated reigning champion Segundo Mercado to win the IBF middleweight championship belt. Over the next six years, he successfully defended his IBF title twenty times without a loss. However, there was still something that eluded Hopkins with all of his success as the IBF champion. There were still two other championship designations (WBA, WBC) middleweight titles that were still held by two other fighters. With three different title belts un-unified, there was no undisputed middleweight champion of the world.

This however changed in 2001, when Hopkins defeated Keith Holmes to win the WBC championship belt. All he needed to do next was to win the WBA title to become the undisputed middleweight champion of the world. On September 29th of that year, Hopkins defeated WBA champion Felix Trinidad and fulfilled Smokey Wilson's prediction by becoming the undisputed middleweight champion of the world. At thirty-six years old, Hopkins made the improbable transition from being one of the youngest inmates in Pennsylvania, to one of the oldest middleweight champions in boxing history.

The year 2001 was scheduled to be the end of his prison sentence, but God saw fit for it to be the arrival time of his destiny instead. It was only through the grace of God that Hopkins happened to serve his time in Graterford, a prison with a boxing program for inmates. The boxing program not only saved his life, but it secured his destiny as well. In 1983 his life may have been headed for frustration and failure, but instead God has used it as a glowing example of inspiration and success.

Bernard Hopkins discovered God's purpose for his life behind prison walls. For some individuals incarceration may be the only way for them to finally focus on what God has placed in them. Other individuals may be trapped behind the personal prison walls of fear, past difficulties and a lack of vision. The same God that elevated Bernard Hopkins is willing and ready to work within your life today. Bernard Hopkins turned his wrinkled and stained canvas into a championship portrait of life turnaround, a fact which is undisputed.

Sylvester Stallone

In March of 1975, Sylvester Stallone was a twenty-eight year old fledgling New York City based actor with less than two hundred dollars to his name. With a few dollars that he previously allocated for entertainment funds, on the 24th of March, he decided to watch the Muhammad Ali/Chuck Wepner fight on closed circuit television. Wepner at the time was a thirty-six year old journeyman fighter, who was given little chance by most boxing observers to pose a legitimate threat to the Heavyweight champion Ali.

In the fight the overmatched Wepner persevered and was able to last a full fifteen rounds with the champion, before losing by unanimous decision, in the eyes of the judges. His lone highlight was the scoring of an improbable knockdown of Ali in the ninth round. Wepner earned the respect of many fight observers including Stallone, by going the distance with the champion.

Inspired by what he witnessed from Wepner, Stallone went straight to work on a script that would both change his life and uplift the world simultaneously. Over a three-day period, Stallone converted his inspiration into action and wrote the script for the film Rocky. It was a story about a washed up boxer named Rocky Balboa, who was surprisingly offered the chance to face the world heavyweight champion Apollo Creed. Just as Wepner did in real life versus Ali, Rocky somehow persevered and beat the odds to last a full fifteen rounds with the champion Creed. Even in defeat just as Wepner did in real life, Rocky earned the respect of boxing observers within the film as well.

The film was released in December 1976 with Stallone playing the title character. Despite being released at the end of the calendar year, it became the highest grossing film that year. The low budget film produced for just over one million dollars went on to earn over 100 million dollars in revenue. It also earned an Academy Award nomination for Stallone and won the Academy Award for best picture in March of 1977.

The success of Rocky spawned the release of five sequels, and made Stallone an internationally respected actor and writer as well. Stallone turned his wrinkled and stained canvas into a cinematic pugilistic masterpiece of universal inspiration. In a three-day period, he changed the course of his life, and placed himself on the correct pathway towards the destiny that God created him to inhabit. With a touch of divine instruction, and a dash of visual inspiration, Stallone turned a life of uncertainty and mediocrity into one of greatness and fulfilled destiny.

Much like his character Rocky, Wepner and the other limitation busters mentioned earlier in this chapter, Stallone was willing to go the distance to live his dreams and fulfill his divine destiny. They all knew that to truly reach their destiny, quitting early would not be permitted. Their tracks through adversity have now become advertisements of achievement attained through perseverance. Each of their once wrinkled and stained canvases have become inspirational masterpieces of human achievement.

There are some of you that were given a clearer canvas to begin life with than others. Somehow over the course of your life, yours may have been wrinkled or stained. You may have had a decent start to your life, but somewhere along the way, you may have ignored or simply forgotten about the tools that God placed within you. Your focus on the masterpiece you were sent to create became disjointed. This loss of focus may have plunged you into the abyss of poverty, drug addiction, criminal activity and other negative conditions of life. It may have caused your canvas design to become negative or unable to be deciphered. It is critical that you realize that there is a God who exists and loves you beyond measure.

There are numerous people that have let a muddled middle of their journey through life confine them to lives filled with negativity, mediocrity, and a chronic lack of achievement. It is incumbent upon everyone to seek God's plan for them through prayer. Even if you feel that your life has turned for the worst, the best that God has to present to you is just around the corner.

The way you escape your confinement is by using the tools God gave you and redesign your life over the wrinkles and stains. You must paint using the colors of God's love, your passion and the belief that you will still create a masterpiece in spite of your circumstances. God gave each of us an abundance of premium quality tools. It must become your mission to complete your masterpiece with them to cover your wrinkled and stained canvas.

Chapter 20 Questions

1. Is the canvas of my life wrinkled and stained?

_____

_____

_____

_____

2. Have I identified the tools within me that I have been blessed to design my canvas with?

_____

_____

_____

_____

3. Have I let the circumstances of my canvas prevent me from designing the masterpiece that God created me to complete?

_____

_____

_____

_____

4. What steps must I take to design over my wrinkled and stained canvas in order to create the masterpiece that God created me to complete?

_____

_____

_____

_____

Chapter 21

The Mental Elements Of Greatness

There are several elements that make up the mental quadrants of greatness. They are the several specific skills that each of us must master in order to fulfill the journey to our destiny. They consist of sacrifice, self-discipline, mental focus, mental filtration, and mental toughness. Each of these mental elements must be combined for us to experience lives of greatness and fulfill our destiny. In this chapter I will explain the importance of each of them.

Sacrifice

For a lot of individuals a missing main ingredient in their recipe for fulfilling their destiny has been sacrifice. Millions of people have let the distraction of multimedia images cost them valuable time in the pursuit of their destiny. Thousands of potential hours of dream building time has been wasted on watching television and surfing the Internet. There is nothing inherently wrong with watching television, or surfing the Internet. The problem with television and Internet is not necessarily the programming we watch, or the sites we browse, but the valuable time we waste gazing at others living their dreams instead of actively pursuing ours. For some the greatest deferment of their destiny has been the distractions of television and the Internet.

The average American watches over twenty hours of television per week. Many of the messages from the airwaves are negative and unconstructive. These messages infiltrate our minds and spirits causing us to detour from the course of our destiny. Just imagine what we could accomplish if we took a fraction of those hours and committed them solely to the building of our dreams.

There is no denying the fact that television and the Internet provide many of us an array of entertainment, news and sports information, which are very important to most of us. The issue is we spend our lives passionate about watching other people revel within their passions, instead of pursuing our own. It turns us from being potential functioning actors in our own lives, to lifetime laboring spectators gazing at other people. We essentially become baked couch potatoes topped with layers of laziness, and sprinkled with a lack of self-discipline. My friends this is why there is no substitute for sacrifice.

Along the pathway to your destiny, there will be things that must be sacrificed. Some of us may have to leave our hometowns and the people that we care about most in pursuit of our destiny. For others your sacrifice may be as simple as cutting down on your unconstructive TV watching and other potential misuses of time that do not benefit the pursuit of your dreams. It is incumbent upon you to determine your personal level of sacrifice in order to create and clear the pathway to your destiny. In order to truly focus on your tasks, the things that could possibly distract you should be minimized or eliminated.

In every area of life, anyone who has ever attained anything worth having has mastered the elements found in the tool of sacrifice. The problem is our society is fueled by the needs of instant satisfaction and gratification. It seems as if many of us desire to attain something for nothing. We tease ourselves with lottery tickets and dreams of instant casino fortunes.

Here is the cold truth; the odds of winning a Mega Millions jackpot are 1 in 175,711,536. The odds of winning a

Powerball jackpot are even higher at 1 in 195,249,054. To put those numbers in perspective, as of 2012, the entire US population was estimated at just over 300 million people.

The odds of being struck by a lightning bolt are nearly twenty times more likely to happen at 1 in 10 million. To put it frankly, depending on the lottery or casino fortunes to grant us the opportunity to live our dreams is pure fallacy. Truthfully most of us would rather wish our way to the shores of destiny as opposed to working our way there.

We must all come to the realization that if anything in this life is worth attaining, our allergic reactions to the necessary work towards it must be cured. Within that work, tough decisions must be made and carried to fruition. For destiny to be reached there are things that must be relinquished. Sacrifice is the prescription that cures the allergic reactions to the required work in the pursuit of our destiny. Just as Jesus Christ gave his life as a sacrifice for the sins of humanity, we must be willing to sacrifice something valuable in order to transform our dreams into reality.

Webster's dictionary defines sacrifice as the surrender of something for the sake of something else. In the pursuit of our destiny, there are three essential elements spawned from sacrifice. They are self-discipline, mental focus and mental toughness. When these three elements work in unison, our sacrifice truly becomes successful. What are you willing to sacrifice?

Self Discipline

The lack of discipline must be sacrificed and a strong layer of self-discipline must replace it on the journey to your destiny. Without self-discipline, nothing you ever set your mind to do would ever be accomplished. Self-discipline is the personal governing system that each of us is blessed with to control our actions. With a strong sense of it, we become self-motivated individuals capable of inspiring ourselves to reach our goals. We each must equip ourselves with a personal system of rules that keeps us adherent and attentive to the dreams within our hearts.

For example, if a person has a goal to lose weight and improve their physical shape, self-discipline is paramount. It is the element that will keep them exercising on a regular basis, and eating the proper healthy foods. It would keep them from resisting the temptations of skipping workouts and eating unhealthy foods deemed counterproductive to their objective. Whenever the individual deviated from their designed weight loss plan, the element of self-discipline would convict them by making them aware of their departure.

The above example about weight loss is simply a microcosm of what our relationships to our unreached destinies represent. There are many of us with the goal of reaching our destiny, but an acute lack of self-discipline has kept us at bay. Our potential lives filled with purposeful living and destiny fulfillment are sacrificed at the expense of a lack of self-discipline.

Instead of cookies and cakes, we eat procrastination and addiction. In place of brownies, we munch on fear and a lack of belief in our abilities. We then drown our unhealthy treats in the milk of discontentment. As opposed to eating candy, we chew on lack of action and are shocked when cavities of disappointment captivate our lives. To top it off, we then refuse to exercise the ambition and promise birthed in our hearts.

The Holy Spirit within us convicts us for our deviations. The evidence of our conviction occurs when the dreams that were planted in our hearts long ago simply refuse to die, no matter how hard we try to contain or kill them. We are then left with an overwhelming feeling of incompleteness within our hearts. When our self- discipline is properly used, it protects us from succumbing to all elements deemed counterproductive to the fulfillment of our destiny.

Many of us look to others to help us stay on task instead of finding the drill sergeant that exists within each of us. For any person to reach their destiny or achieve anything worth attaining in this life, they must become disciples of their own personal mantras of self-discipline. It is imperative that you take the time to hold yourself accountable for your own actions and inactions as well. It is critical that you exercise your muscles of faith and claim the purpose and destiny on your life. Self-discipline allows the focus aimed squarely on your goals to overcome the circumstances of your existence.

In our society, the art of delayed gratification has been replaced by the abstract of instant satisfaction. This trend must be reversed in order to allow your dreams to manifest into fulfilled destiny. If you depend on someone else to provide the discipline you need, you will wind up waiting your whole life and still not receive it. It is the equivalent of expecting a city bus or taxi to pick you up in the midst of a winter blizzard. It is simply an unreliable set of circumstances.

We are all individually responsible for the infrastructure of our dreams and their safe transit to fulfillment at the shores of destiny. It is only through our self-discipline that we will reach our destiny on schedule regardless of whatever happens around us. Self-discipline allows each of us to awaken daily with the focus of what we will become despite what we presently are or previously were. It keeps our eye on the prize when other factors vie for our attention.

The lack of self-discipline has placed scores of people within the unfriendly confines of addiction. Addiction takes on several forms including: drug, alcohol, sexual, food, television and internet. All addictions are the result of an acute lack of self-discipline within our lives. No one puts a gun to our heads and forces us to excessively engage in any of the destiny robbing behaviors mentioned above.

Self-discipline equips you to win the battle versus peer pressure and societal expectations. Self-discipline sets personal standards, which monitor exactly what is best for you and how much of it is in your best interest. The level of self-discipline you possess keeps you within moderation standards that you feel are most appropriate for your life.

There are millions of people who set standards of self-discipline for their lives but simply do not follow them. They try to please other people or attempt to look important to others and often wind up wondering why things don't seem to go their way. You must not live to people please but instead seek to please God. To accomplish this you must create a personal set of standards that align with the will of God for your life.

Once you create a set of standards for your life, you must live by them with no exceptions to your rules. When you acquiesce by bending or breaking your rules, it leaves the door open to distracting elements deemed detrimental to your destiny. There must be dedication to the cause of disciplining yourself. A majority of the ills of our society and the chronic lack of destiny fulfillment plaguing our world are rooted in the malady known as lack of self-discipline.

Many of us pay far too much attention to the standards that our peer groups and society attempts to impose on us. So many of us get caught up attempting to live up to their standards that we neglect to create or live by our own. We stand for nothing and wind up falling for everything that becomes readily accessible to us. The cowardly follower who lives to please people over God's will for our lives replaces the fearless leader in each of us. This way of living must end for us to truly walk in the greatness of God. Left unchecked, peer and societal pressures are elements that cause many dreams to burst and destinies to evaporate. Take comfort in knowing that self-discipline is the security mechanism that protects your dreams from the wanton elements deemed notorious for destroying dreams.

For some people it may be difficult to say no to getting drunk, high or kicking other addictions. I also equally understand that it maybe difficult for some to moderate and monitor their use of television and Internet. Are any of these items worth forfeiting your destiny for? For someone reading this right now, one of the above items could be keeping your destiny at bay.

Living within our own skin is an individual experience that we all face daily. We are each the captains of our own journey via the free will that God blessed us with to make choices. Self-discipline was included within the package of free will and when it is left unapplied; our lives will be tethered to security, mediocrity and failure. It is not the responsibility of God, society, or our peers to impose self-discipline in our lives. It is the task of the individual who glances back at each of us in the mirror. When you take control of your own behavior, you simultaneously make your path to destiny more transparent.

The time has come for each of us to take back control of our lives. The potential destiny that God has planned for each of our lives is too important to be blown on a technicality such as a lack of self-discipline. We must stand up for our lives and step up to the destiny that awaits us. It is not my aim to come off as overly critical or pastoral, but to only be honest about the virtues and benefits of self-discipline. When we engage in and apply the art of self-discipline, it reveals to God and society our level of earnestness in our quest to reach the shores of our destiny.

Mental Focus

The third element in the quadrant of greatness is mental focus. Mental focus is the sworn enemy of laziness and distractions. When you establish whatever goal you eventually would like to accomplish, your ability to mentally focus is critical. It represents your ability to stay focused on accomplishing the dreams within your heart. An individual who is mentally focused is someone who is not easily distracted. They live daily with the fierce determination to let nothing detrimental to their goals knock them off course. They understand that distractions are a part of life, but their level of focus does not allow them to interfere with the accomplishment of their goals.

For mental focus to be effective, there must first be an object of desire to be focused on. For example, take the dream of someone who desires to be a first time homeowner. If someone had the dream of owning a new home, there would be several factors that they would need to work in unison for them.

The first step would be identifying the house they desire. The second step once they have selected the house would be for the potential homeowner to obtain financing for their purchase. Traditionally, the prospective homeowner would have saved approximately ten to twenty percent cash as a down payment toward the principle cost of their home. For example if the home they desired cost 200,000 dollars, the prospective buyer would need to come up with between twenty to forty thousand dollars for the down payment of their home.

If the prospective buyer is truly serious about owning a home, the individual will make sure that they would save enough money to cover the down payment amount. Their mental focus is supported by self- discipline, which would force them to eliminate unnecessary purchases, which would subtract funds from their down payment goal. They would then refrain from spending their earmarked funds on things such as a car, jewelry or clothing just to name a few examples. Their ability to remain focused on their dream of future homeownership would be the driving force behind their need to save for a substantial down payment. They would come to the understanding that in order to make their dream of homeownership a reality, a down payment must be committed.

A second example of applied mental focus would be an example of an individual with aspirations of becoming a Medical Doctor. If a person aspired to become a Medical Doctor, their college undergraduate major would not be History or Sociology. Even though History and Sociology are fine majors they would not serve the proper purpose of preparing the individual for a career in medicine.

A college undergraduate student with a goal of becoming a Medical Doctor would most likely major Pre-Med in fields such as Biology or Chemistry. These disciplines would lay a solid foundation for the individual in their preparation for medical school. Majoring in disciplines unrelated to medicine could possibly be attractive to the student, but would not help facilitate their goal of becoming a Medical Doctor.

Their level of mental focus would serve as a daily reminder of their goal to become a Medical Doctor and not a Historian or Sociologist. They are not distracted from their goal by other elements that may vie for their attention. Once their goal is established, their mental focus will let nothing interfere with its eventual fulfillment.

For someone reading this a lack of mental focus has kept your destiny at bay in your life. Many of us set goals to attain the dreams of our heart, but we let our level of mental focus relax and thus became distracted by items unrelated to our dreams. We dealt with the distractions for so long that many of us simply gave up on the dreams within our hearts or refused to acknowledge their existence. It is important that we remember that our levels of self-discipline and mental focus work together. Self-discipline is the foundation that supports the weight of our mental focus.

There are millions of individuals who left high school or college with dreams in their hearts. They left school full of energy and life ready to take on the world and transform their dreams into reality. The problem happened when they left school, most of them left with various bills with their names on them. They then felt the need to get a decent job to help pay the bills they accumulated. When this happened they took their dreams and abandoned them in order to survive economically.

At this point they exchanged the potential to live and work for meaning, for the reality of existing and working for money. They entered the rat race and watched their dreams crushed beneath the weight of its wheel. Days turned into weeks, weeks into months and months into years. During that time period their mental focus changed from making their dreams come true, to making sure they paid whatever bill was due.

A great number of them got married and/or had children and assumed that the reality of the rat race lifestyle was all that they were created to experience on earth. They convinced themselves that dreams were for children or for individuals other than them. They told people stories about how much promise their life once had and often reminisced over previous happiness in the years of their youth. Their mental focus became centered on everyday problems instead of potential solutions for them. Their dreams now consist of hitting the lottery or maybe getting the chance to take their children or grandchildren to Disney World.

The problem now for many of people as the years have passed by, is that the dream that was crushed underneath the wheel of the rat race still haunts them. As they go to their jobs every day it becomes harder to get out of bed. They have come to the realization that they have essentially traded in a life filled with potential creativity for one filled with daily robotic repetition.

They employ their mental focus by making deals with themselves to make it through the grinding days, weeks, months and years of their life. They check the lottery numbers every Friday night hoping that luck will see fit to become their liberator. They hit the racetrack looking for a superfecta. Many of them even hit the casino or the bingo hall praying to God for their numbers to fall. They spend their lives wishing and praying for monetary riches instead of working toward excavating the treasure trove in their hearts. The place where their dormant gifts, talents and dreams lay scattered.

Are you one of the people that I just described? If so things can change for you today. Life is a short production that does not contain any sequels in the works. No matter how old you are and how long ago you let your dreams die, it is never too late to resuscitate the dreams in your heart. Today, I am your ghostbuster and the time has come to turn the dreams that haunt you into the reality that awaits you.

Just as easily as your mental focus changed years earlier, it can still be changed back by simply substituting the desires of your debtors for the dreams within your heart. God never put dreams in our hearts, to let the circumstances of the world crush them. There is still time to pick up the broken pieces of your dreams, put them back together and place them in the framework of your destiny. There is no need to worry if the frame is the correct size for your reconnected pieces. Before you were born the frame maker (God) also created the pieces of your dreams to customly fit within the framework of your destiny. The creator left no space in the framework for a lack of mental focus, a lack of self-discipline or laziness to occupy any room.

No journey to destiny is completed without the aide of mental focus. There is someone reading this who grasps this concept but are just plain lazy in applying it. Laziness has scores of people with first place potential lagging behind in a last place life, in the quest to reach their destiny. Laziness leads directly to procrastination, which leads to a destiny delayed or ultimately unfulfilled. It is the task of your self-discipline to arrest the spirit of laziness and imprison it behind the stone walls of ambition.

For others, it may not have been bills that sent your dreams off track but the unsupportive words of your family members or friends in regards to the dreams within you. Sometimes the individuals closest to us are the people that we allow to compromise our level of mental focus. We let the plan they have for our lives outweigh the plans of our self and God.

There must come a point in your life when you must make sure that your dreams reflect the desires of your heart and are not the dreams that someone else has for you. There are millions of individuals currently living frustrated and non-purpose driven lives, because they made decisions contrary to the desires of their heart. They refused to stand up for the dreams of their hearts and settled for the suggestions of those closest to them.

There is someone reading this currently that may have been led by God to go into the arts but were instead persuaded to go into a completely unrelated field at the behest of those closest to them. There is someone else who had the dream and vision of becoming an entrepreneur but was instead persuaded to play life safe and settle for life seeking work and economic security. There are young women out there who were pushed by their families into marrying men for financial security, rather than the sanctity of love.

Years later many of these people look back on their decisions with regret wondering how different their lives could have been if they had only listened to their inner voice. These examples prove precisely why your level of mental focus is so critical. When you have a strong sense of mental focus, you will make decisions that are in your best interest regardless of who is pressuring you or whatever obstacles lay ahead of you.

Ultimately, you must live with the decisions that you make, regardless of their future outcome. It is up to you to know the dreams of your heart and own them. There are many parents and other loved ones who try to live their unfulfilled dreams through your life. They mean well in their intentions but are often wrong in their assertions.

Many of us have made the critical error of forfeiting our own identities, to fit the images of what other people feel that our lives should resemble. Pleasing these well meaning individuals is fine when it comes to areas of morals or values but not when it comes to the areas of dreams and destiny. The areas concerning the dreams of your heart and your destiny are a sacred place to be shared only between God and you.

Mental Filtering

In the same manner that not all combinations of fruits and vegetables are best for you, not all advice or life suggestions imparted from others is in the best interest of your dreams. Not all advice is great advice even from the people you reciprocate your love to. You must learn to discern beneficial and non-beneficial input from those closest to you. This area is where your ability to mentally filter comes into play. It is the fourth element in the mental quadrant of greatness. Each of us is equipped with the ability to utilize the information that others give us and discard the information that is not applicable to our lives. It is vitally important to keep the treasure and discard the trash.

The reason that so many people are off track is due to neglecting to use, or clear and clean out their mental filters. The process is similar to using a power juicer to make drinks out of fruits and vegetables. The role of the filter in the power juicer is to take the fruits and vegetables, grind out their pulp and extract its nutritious juice for us to enjoy. If the filter were not in place, we would have drinks filled with non-essential chunks of pulp in addition to whatever amount of juice was produced. The result would be a drink that fails to taste like we anticipated it would.

When the filter is not cleared and cleaned out, and used continuously, the drinks that are produced will not taste how we expect them to. This is because there are left over particles from previously made concoctions. These previous particles are only cleared away when the filter is cleansed. The ultimate results of us not using our filter, or not keeping it cleared and cleaned are confusion of taste buds, a clogged machine and utter disappointment in the quality of drink we produce.

There are some individuals that have neglected to filter out the imparted information of others. To their own detriment, they have kept everything thrown their way and received very little of what they really needed. Others neglected to clear and clean out their mental filters and eventually became confused and mentally convoluted with lingering thoughts that should have been previously discarded.

A great number of people unfortunately took the advice of everyone but themselves. They aspired to be everything that others wanted them to be, instead of what God called them to be. Knowing when and what to filter out of your train of thought play a major role in keeping your dreams on track and your level of mental focus intact. There are too many people who look back on their lives lamenting the fact that their lack of proper mental filtration caused them to make decisions that were not in their best interest. Many of us blame our parents or other loved ones for pressuring us to do things that we knew contradicted the desires of our hearts. We blame them for our lack of dream fulfillment, when we are the true culprits.

We are the only ones in charge of our mental focus including the information we filter in and out. The lack of mental focus and filtration has caused scores of individuals with million dollar intellect to settle for thousand dollar jobs, hundred dollar relationships and ten cent qualities of life. There is no point in going back over your life and blaming other people for influencing decisions in your life, especially when you possessed the ultimate power to make them.

It is imperative that you use those past experiences as learning tools and reference points for future situations. We all must realize that when we are mentally focused, our mental filters work at their optimum levels. This is essential for both destiny fulfillment and for enjoying life locked in the zone of greatness.

In the area of athletics the common thread of any great NFL football quarterback, MLB baseball hitter, NBA basketball or NHL hockey scorer is their level of mental focus. They all deal with the pressures of performing at the highest levels in their respective sports. They also learn to cope with the pressure from the crowds and deal with defenders that may distract them.

The thing that separates the great ones from the good and mediocre ones is their ability to master the speed of the game. If you ask any athlete at which point was their success greatest, they will unanimously say whenever the game slowed down to them. For when the game slowed down, it allowed them to make concise decisions no matter what their surrounding circumstances were. This state of being is what I refer to as the zone of greatness.

The zone of greatness is open to anyone who strives to become great in any walk of life, not just athletics. It is the place where your mental focus, mental filtration and decision making function at your highest capabilities. It is also where your gifts and talents begin to flourish, because all potential distractions are impeded by the strong force of your mental focus.

In the case of the athletes, what separated them on every level from high school to the professional level was their ability to dominate the speed of the game at all levels. When the game truly slows down, the great athletes operate at a pace one step ahead of everyone else, instead of two steps behind struggling to keep pace.

Our lives are very similar to that of the great athletes. The problem is in life, many of us have not had the experience of our viewpoints of life slowing down. Our levels of mental focus are wasted, wondering and worrying about elements that are out of our control.

A large number of us fixate on the pressures of life and the obstacles it places in our path. When we do this we fall behind the curve in the quest for our destiny and we wind up on the treadmill of life expeditiously running nowhere. We then yield the power of our mental focus and decision making to the obstacles we face and the pressures we endure. This intrusion of distraction robs us of the opportunity to experience life in the zone of greatness and instead imposes to us a life sentence of struggle and disappointment.

The way to slow down the speed of life is through increasing your level of mental focus on the positive things that you would like to see take place. The next step is to identify your distractions and either control them, or eliminate them completely from your life. To accomplish this, you must tap into the power of the Holy Spirit that resides in you. God's Holy Spirit gives you not only the strength to battle against your distractions, but also the power to make the proper decisions for your life when you feel that you are not strong enough to do so. It is a valuable God given natural resource that a great number of people fail to utilize.

Once the speed of life slows down your mental focus will become clearer and your level of decision making will operate at its capable capacity. This will then uncover your gifts and talents and permit them to operate in the zone of greatness. Then and only then will your life truly operate at a pace one step ahead of life instead of two steps behind, or at its same pace. When you dominate the speed of life and its pace slows down to you, you will enjoy both Kingdom and world success simultaneously. In the same manner that you choose faith over fear, you must choose firm mental focus over any and all distractions. The future of your destiny demands it.

Mental Toughness

The fifth and final element in the mental quadrant of greatness is mental toughness. It is the combination of mental strength and mental perseverance. The truth is life's coldest realities and difficult circumstances have the ability to turn the mightiest of men and women into meek quitters. Mental fatigue has the ability to turn anyone of us into cowards if we allow it to. This is only possible when we make the decision to place more stock in our difficult situations, than we place in discovering solutions for them. Each person must answer the question, how much can I withstand?

For any person to reach the shores of destiny, possessing thick skin is a prerequisite. Both self-discipline and mental focus are the adhesive makeup that sustains mental toughness. When your mental toughness is used to its full capacity you tend to eschew quitting on the object of your mental focus. It equips you with the strength to hold on to your self-discipline no matter what distractions may tug at you. Mental toughness is the fabric that separates champions from contenders and is the fruit of confidence.

Your journey to destiny is essentially a battle of wits that takes place between life and you. It is a place where the solidity of your mental toughness is tested daily. Without mental toughness, life will pound you into submission. As human beings our plight is similar to that of a boxer fighting for an opportunity to be crowned the champion of the world and someday later be admitted into Boxing's Hall of Fame.

In life we are all fighters facing life in the battle to go the distance to our destiny. Millions of individuals allow life to get the best of them in the early rounds on their pathway to destiny. They take a couple of hard blows from life and they forget what they were fighting for in the first place. They neglect to listen to the advice of the head trainer (God) and wonder why they continue to get pummeled by blows that threaten to knock them out. Some quit and others simply refuse to give their best effort. Round after round they lean on life, refuse to punch back and hope the bell will save them. They struggle to survive without an attack plan.

In order to be victorious and go the distance, we must all humble ourselves and heed the instructions of our training staff. They are made up of God, Jesus and the Holy Spirit. They have never lost a fight. They see things that we cannot see from their viewpoint in our corner. They inform us of our best defensive strategies that allow us to shield and deflect the blows life will throw at us.

They also inform us of the best methods of offense for us to attack life before it attacks us and teach us the sweet science of counterpunching after it attacks us. After each round we are refilled and refreshed by our trainer with the living water of his Holy Spirit. Any cuts and abrasions we absorb, our cutman Jesus soothes and covers our wounds with the healing balm of Gilead.

In our daily lives our post round trips to our corner represent our times of prayer, fellowship and the study of God's word. It is where we are recharged, coached and strengthened to fight life to the distance. How well we defend ourselves in the fight with life determines two things. The first thing it determines is if we are fit to earn our destiny by going the distance. The second thing it determines is if we are fit to ultimately enter the Kingdom of Heaven when our fighting days are finished.

The solidity of our defense is tested by life's situations. How well we offensively attack and counterpunch determines the quality of life we experience while on earth. They encompass our mental, physical and spiritual standards of living. Not necessarily the amount of money we earn or how popular we are on earth as some of us may hope. At some point in our battle, we must discover that it is always better to have an indefinite amount of peace of mind, than a definite amount of world recognition.

To happily reach our destiny, we must possess a combination of mental toughness and peace of mind regardless of our financial circumstances. Notice I did not say financial riches lead to happiness. On this earth there is no disputing the fact that we all need money to help create suitable standards of personal living. I refer to money as a measure of societal stamina, which sustains us on our feet in our fight with life. Each of us has the ability to gain societal stamina through the usage of our gifts and talents that our corner blessed us with.

Some individuals may have as much or more societal stamina than others, but they will not go the distance because they do not share the same training staff that guides us. Others may share our training staff, but they fail to heed the instructions that the corner provides to them. They choose to battle on their own without the aid of the divine training staff. These individuals sustain unnecessary punishment that prevents them from going the distance to their destiny.

Our level of peace of mind fuels mental toughness. No matter what we may face our peace of mind provides us with enough mental toughness to sustain our strength and not allow us to quit in the face adversity. Peace of mind is developed during our training sessions.

Our training sessions are the times in our lives when our training staff has previously proved their value to us on countless occasions. These are the times we look back on and know with all certainty that it was nothing but the grace of our head trainer that helped us move on. The times we look back on equip us with the confidence to face anything that life sends our way head on.

The living water of the Holy Spirit is the spiritual anointing that keeps our peace of mind optimized. We keep our water refreshed daily through worship, obedience, positive thinking and Godly actions. It is truly the boost we need to guide and sustain us at a championship level in our battle versus life.

When we eventually battle through the fight and make it the distance, our destiny awaits us. When we win enough fights, our corner extends us an invitation to their Hall of Fame better known as Heaven. Our purse was funded by our cutman Jesus, who gave his earthly life on a wooden cross nearly two thousand years ago. His sacrifice granted each of us the opportunity to reach earthly glory at our destiny and receive heavenly glory when our final bell has tolled.

In our battle versus life, none of us are made aware of the number of rounds we have individually been granted to wage battle in. Some individuals may be granted more rounds than others. Only our training staff truly knows the answer to that enigma. Each round we battle in could potentially be our last one that we have an opportunity to face life in. This is precisely why it is imperative that we follow the instructions of our corner and fight each round as if it were our last.

We can all take comfort in the fact that our trainers gave us the necessary tools and training needed to make it through as many rounds required to go the distance. They understood that our ability to mentally endure would keep us going strong when others were fainting in the face of obstacles and difficult circumstances.

The only way we can go the distance is to take the tools and training we have been given and apply them with every fiber of our being. There are far too many people that let their levels of mental weakness allow the vicissitudes of life destroy their dreams. They then refuse to fight or quit in the midst of battle. This can be overcome by simply remembering that our trainers have given us all the preparation we will ever need to go the distance. They know how much we can deal with and how much we can deal out.

To go the distance, the training that once toughened our minds must then become the truth that sustains us in our fight. We must know that our trainers didn't spend the time to toughen us, for us to simply quit when the battle got tough. They knew what our destiny had the potential to be before they began training us. It is our responsibility to follow through on our potential and make them proud to have produced another champion and future member of Heaven's Hall of Fame.

Chapter 21 Questions

1. Is a lack of sacrifice costing me the opportunity to fulfill my destiny? If so how must I improve?

_____

_____

_____

_____

2. Is a lack of self-discipline keeping my destiny at bay? If so how must I improve?

_____

_____

_____

_____

3. Is a lack of mental focus keeping my destiny captive from me? If so how must I improve?

_____

_____

_____

_____

4. Is a lack of mental filtration keeping my destiny captive from me? If so how must I improve?

_____

_____

_____

_____

5. Is a lack of mental toughness responsible for my destiny being unfulfilled? If so how must I improve?

_____

_____

_____

_____

Chapter 22

There Is A Buyer For What You Sell

How much are you worth? What is your value to both God and society? When I ask these questions it is not in relation to monetary net worth or public opinions about your life. It is an introspection of sorts that should push you to seek the meaning of your life. Many of us forget that we are the children of God. Also known as the King of Glory who reigns and resides in the Kingdom of Heaven. This revelation means that each of us are royal heirs in the greatest monarchy of all, the Kingdom of God.

All over the world people have unknowingly traded in their potential lives as princes and princesses for lives as existential paupers. Their lives as paupers are not necessarily reflected in their financial statements, but instead are revealed in the verbal statements they make to themselves, and in their physical applications that display their pauper like mentalities.

If you fail to recognize the value of your life, the world will assign a value to you. The world's values are assigned in the form of labels. God's value is assigned through his favor, which is manifested through your gifts, talents and blessings. There is someone on earth that can reap the benefits of the value that you sow. Each living person is a valuable asset to the Kingdom of God.

When you traverse through life unaware of your value, you will often settle for situations beneath your worth. It is imperative that you recognize that your mind and body are valuable gifts from God that you must treat as sacred real estate. There are scores of individuals with high levels of self-respect that are simultaneously unaware of their value.

Knowing your value is the key to living a purpose driven life in a money driven world. Your sense of value gives you a reason to arise from your bed every day. When you know your value, you will live your life with a specific purpose in mind instead of wandering aimlessly through it. Each and every one of us is a valuable asset to God. We were all sent to earth to fulfill a specific God ordained purpose. Without the knowledge of our purpose we are rendered as lost individuals existing and lacking life direction.

Your true self can only be uncovered when your purpose for living is revealed. If you lack the knowledge of your purpose, your self-value cannot be quantified. This causes scores of people to go through life unsure of what they are qualified for. This leads to the weight of personal certainty becoming null and void in their decision making and causes them to make decisions based on the value that others assign to their lives.

In your discovery of your value, you must know who you belong to before you can truly understand who you are. This happens when a person makes the decision to fall back in love with pleasing God, as opposed to satisfying their personal capitalistic desires or those of others. When someone makes the decision to please God with their way of living, it opens the door for their purpose and destiny to be revealed. Each of us must discover what we mean to our Heavenly Father and validate his decision to place us on earth. As you discover who you are, you must learn to accept the findings and uncover the fabric of comfort in relation to your own uniqueness.

In his first letter to the Corinthians chapter 7 verses 22-24, the Apostle Paul extols the virtue of our value. He states, "For he who is called in the Lord while a slave is the Lord's freedman. Likewise he who is called while free is Christ's slave. You were bought at a price; do not become slaves of men. Brethren, let each one remain with God in that state in which he was called." This shows us that no matter what label society may impart on us it all pales in comparison to our calling. You belong to Christ and are the property of God as a result of the price that Jesus paid on the cross. The virtues of your value must be understood in order for you to merit the full benefits of your calling.

As children of God the time has come for us to remove the makeup of lies and daydreaming and exfoliate our lives with the compounds of truth and reality. Each of us must truthfully find a way to answer the questions: Who am I, how did I get here, and which direction is my life headed? Only we can answer these questions in reference to the current state of our own lives. It is a wonderful example of the gift of free will that God presented each of us with to make the vital decisions that govern our lives.

A great number of individuals spend their whole lives searching for money in everything, and neglect to discover the meaning of anything. This is best illustrated in the career choices of millions of unhappy Americans. Many of us have let our quest for the largest possible monetary value guide our focus, and have simultaneously lost track of our own level of value. This is done because the world convinces us that societal happiness and our personal levels of value are rooted in money and socioeconomic status. For a lot of people their greatest mistake has been the single-minded pursuit of the fruits of societal happiness. It has led some to feelings of happiness, but also has left many more individuals feeling and living incomplete lives.

The fruits of societal happiness however, are not enough to complete the true picture of value. Since we are the rightful heirs of God's Kingdom, the fruits of societal happiness are rendered impotent in their attempt to complete our lives. Since we are the heirs of God, we must choose to seek Kingdom happiness above societal happiness. Kingdom happiness is rooted in the unyielding fibers of love. The true value that God placed within us is only revealed through the power of love.

The power of love is the networking mechanism that connects each of us to one another and to the inhabitants of Heaven. To achieve any true level of God given success, love must be present. Without love, there can be no measurable level of true happiness. Scores of individuals have earnestly searched for love in the wrong places and unknowingly diminished their value in the process. They seek it from variants such as money, their occupations and anything or anyone that makes them feel accepted. They choose to define their human value in the comfort of material goods and elements that provide temporary comfort for long-term circumstances.

To change this, we must all seek to uncover the value of God's love for us. This is accomplished when we attempt to see ourselves from his perspective in relation to us. Once this is accomplished, we will then understand what each of our values to humanity represent. There are six components that represent the equation of True Human Value when they are combined. I have listed them below in the order of their importance.

Knowing and understanding that God loves you
Loving and honoring God
Loving yourself
Loving other people
Receiving love from other people
Imparting love into your daily tasks

The six components of human value each represent branches on the tree of value. This tree is at its best when it is rooted in the fertile soil of God's love and will for our lives. There must be equal balance between the six elements for us to measure our true value to humanity. Each person must determine the fair market value of their own life. You must know with certainty exactly how much your stock is worth within the great stock exchange known as life. You must be able to answer each of the questions below?

1. Is my value appreciating or depreciating?
2. What kind of dividends do I produce for those that come in contact with me?
3. Am I a blue chip or a junk bond?

The answers to these questions are just a couple of the factors that will help you determine your true value to humanity. Within each of us are the gifts and talents that our fellow inhabitants of humanity need. We are all valuable assets to the Kingdom of God and humanity. It may take time, but it is imperative that you find your designated position within the ever-changing puzzle of life.

Lifetime Value Guarantee

If I made the decision to take a bag filled with gold and platinum coins and dumped them at the bottom of the ocean, would the coins lose their value? The answer is a resounding no. Even if the bag of coins were left at the bottom of the ocean for decades or centuries, their value would remain intact. This is possible because when the elements were created; they were equipped with special components that prevented their possible oxidation from elements such as water.

They were created with the highest possible components bestowed upon metals. These special components assured their ability to withstand time and any adverse circumstances that may have surrounded them. It does not matter how many years they were surrounded by circumstances non-conducive to their purpose, because their value would not diminish or disappear. Whenever they are rediscovered, they will still be as valuable as the day when they were originally created.

Our lives bear a resemblance to that of the gold and platinum coins. Even though many of us have lost our sense of value over the years, it has never and will never depreciate. When God created us, he equipped us with components that safeguarded our value from depreciation and disappearance, no matter what we are currently or previously have been surrounded by. The fact that you may have spent years surrounded by elements non-conducive to your purpose does not matter. Your value still remains as high as the day you were born.

The fact that God loved each of us enough to give us an opportunity to live is proof of our value to him. Since he rewarded us with a chance to live and eventually join him, we must validate his decision to send us to earth. To validate his choice we must discover our value and learn to live our lives both in and on purpose seeking to fulfill our destiny. We must choose to live righteously instead of conforming to popular standards of accepted societal living. To reach the shores of destiny, each of us must know our value and strive to live lives that reflect our knowledge of it.

Chapter 22 Questions

1. What is the fair market value of my life?

_____

_____

_____

_____

2. Is the lack of knowledge of my value keeping my destiny away from me?

_____

_____

_____

_____

3. What are the instruments by which I measure my value?

_____

_____

_____

_____

4. Do I understand my value to both God and humanity?

_____

_____

_____

_____

5. Have I attempted to view my life from God's perspective
and if so what does it tell me?

_____

_____

_____

_____

PART FIVE

Friday

DATE WITH DESTINY

Chapter 23

The Shores of Destiny

The shores of destiny are the place where we use what God has specifically placed in us to enrich society. It is a place in which our service honors God by using our unique blends of gifts and talents to the best of our abilities. He placed those unique blends within us as a means by which to both honor him and serve the world as a whole. It is the place where we fulfill God's designed purpose for our lives. It is the place where the power of love and service outweighs the pull of money and societal status. Destiny is the place that God created for us with the intention of each of us reaching it.

Some of us may reach and inhabit it in our youthful years; others will reach it at a later date in our lives. It does not matter when you arrive, as long as you arrive before you pass away from this earth. In his first letter to the Corinthians chapter 12 verses 4-7 the Apostle Paul states, "There are diversities of gifts, but the same Spirit. There are differences of ministries, but the same Lord. And there are diversities of activities, but it is the same God who works all in all. But the manifestation of the Spirit is given to each one for the profit of all."

This lets us know both the power and importance of the proper usage of our gifts and talents. It also tells that our gifts are to be used for us to work together with others in order to strengthen God's Kingdom. We are all given different gifts, but in order for them to work to their full capacity, we must all work together united under the umbrella of God's will.

The Importance of Destiny

For some your arrival at the shores may bring you financial riches in the eyes of the world. I cannot guarantee that for everyone, but I can guarantee spiritual riches beyond measure for all. Those that may not have financial riches waiting for them will still reap the rewards of a mission well done. Awaiting the arrival of everyone is a level of peace of mind unmatched by any monetary amount. Destiny is the home of both functioning actors and actors emeritus. When you make the decision to leave the land of security and swim through the currents of fear and across the sea of mediocrity, you will reach the shores of destiny. The shores of destiny are the location where dreams of future possibilities are exchanged for the reality of what was once imagined.

Many people may question, why is it important for me to reach the shores of destiny? The answer is simple; it is because when you reach your destiny you validate the gift of God's decision to place you on earth. You transition from being a cog in a machine to being a solution to a problem. Each life on earth is designed and purposed to advance the movement of the Kingdom of God. Each one of us provides an answer to the questions of someone else.

Most of the inhabitants of the shores of destiny are not famous entertainment stars or business tycoons. Its inhabitants are comprised of mostly ordinary individuals that have lived and continue to live extraordinary lives. Your safe passage to the shores of destiny cannot be purchased or negotiated it must be earned. It is earned through the sweat equity accumulated during the process of deciphering your purpose, and by you making the conscious decision to illuminate the light of God through your faithful works. This is done through your words, thoughts and actions. Whenever you speak, it should sound like God talking through you.

Whenever you think, your thoughts should reflect a God like mentality and whenever you walk, it should appear as if God walks beside you.

Before you can earn anything, including a life promotion or the attainment of your destiny, you must first seek the Kingdom of God. As you seek the Kingdom you must strive to earnestly live as righteously as you can. In the book of Matthew chapter 6 verse 33 Jesus states, "But seek ye first the Kingdom of God and his righteousness, and all these things shall be added unto you." The reason that you must first seek the desires of God and his righteousness is because there are no blessings granted without the grace of God.

When you live within God's designed purpose, the world can see his light through the fruits of your work. When this happens you prove to God that you honor him for blessing you with the gifts and talents that he saw fit to equip you with. It allows you to shine brightly alone from what may be popular to the world sometimes, but popular with God at all times.

Destiny is the place where you submit to the will of God for your life by fully operating in your gifts. It is the grace of God that sustains your operations. The Apostle Paul addresses this matter in his letter to the Ephesians chapter 4 verses 7-8. He states, "But to each one of us grace was given according to the measure of Christ's gift. Therefore He says: When he ascended on high he led captivity captive and gave gifts to men."

At your point of destiny, you no longer live for Friday and dread Sunday night. You no longer simply exist by going through the motions of life from Sunday night until Friday afternoon. Each day is lived to the fullest of life, and lends itself as a showcase for the exhibition of your life's purpose. It is the point when you wake up every day fully knowing that the anointed hand of God covers and moves you as if you were pieces on a chessboard.

The space of hours between the time you arise and the time you sleep are filled with activities that display both the desires of your heart and the will of God for your life. It is where your work will not feel like a job to pay the bills, but rather a calling that helps to fulfill your life's purpose. It is where you can be compensated financially for doing what you are most passionate about. It is a task that you would do for free if money was not needed as a means to survive in our world.

There is a task that fits this description for each of us. It calls to us through the channel of our hearts, which is where God speaks to us. When we make the decision to place the desires of our hearts first, it keeps us within the correct state of being. It permits love to lead us into a place of happiness that cannot be purchased. As I alluded to earlier, the shores of destiny may not contain financial riches for each of us. It does however offer everyone the opportunity for financial comfort, peace of mind and an escape from the survival mode that many of us have unfortunately only ever known.

Everyday living on the shores of destiny will not be absent of disappointment or heartache. There will still be the same situations and circumstances that life places in the path of anyone. The major difference now is that you will be equipped with the agents of perspective and peace of mind to illuminate your trek through the darkest points of your life. You will possess the strength to navigate through anything simply because our Father in Heaven has given each of us the power of his Holy Spirit to be more than conquerors.

There is so much more room for more people to transition to the shores of destiny. It is a place that God specifically created for us to walk within his power during our time on this earth. It is never too late to get there, no matter what may have precluded you from reaching it sooner. You must believe that you will get there and take the necessary steps to ensure your safe passage to it. There is honestly no excuse for not doing your best to make it there. When you do your part, God will take care of the rest. Jesus did not give his life for us to simply pass through life and hope for Heaven to answer our call. We were sent here to earn our way into Heaven through our bodies of earthly work. Reaching the shores of destiny is a highlight each of us should strive to include on our resume of life.

Where Is Destiny?

Many people may wonder where the shores of destiny are located. The truth is it cannot be found on a globe or on a world atlas. The shores of destiny are not a fictitious place in a far away strange land. This slice of Heaven on earth is not found at an exclusive island resort either. Its geographical coordinates are located within the latitude of our minds, and in the longitude of our hearts. When those two points intersect and God's Holy Spirit is in the midst, it equates to the point of our prime meridians of fulfilled destiny being reached.

The guiding force that pushes us to the pinnacle of God's plan for our lives must be and can only be love. Love is the singular form of infrastructure that sustains the shores of destiny. Dreams dissipate, people pass away and money fades, but only love can withstand any test that the hands of time may send its way. It is the greatest gift that God has placed in us and it allows each of us the opportunity to reflect him through us.

In his first letter to the Corinthians chapter 13 verses 1-3 the Apostle Paul states, "Though I speak with the tongues of men and of angels, but have not love, I have become sounding brass or a clanging cymbal. And though I have the gift of prophecy, and understand all mysteries and all knowledge, and though I have all faith, so that I could remove mountains, but have not love, I am nothing. And though I bestow all my goods to feed the poor, and though I give my body to be burned, but have not love, it profits me nothing."

The Apostle Paul illustrates the point that without love, our God given gifts and talents are essentially useless. The power of love is the supply source for the strength of our gifts. God ultimately proved his love for us when he sent his son Jesus to earth, to die for our right to eternal life and obtain salvation from sin. He then took matters one step further with his decision to send us to earth with unique gifts and talents to build up his Kingdom on earth. Each of us was chosen out of God's love. We all have a job to do and fortunately for us whomever God calls he also equips. When we reach the shores of destiny with the aid of love, we truly fulfill our mission to the best of our abilities.

Our lives are far too precious a gift to go through them and neglect to reach the shores of our destiny. As long as there is breath in our lungs, the opportunity still exists. The time has come for each of us to become all that God has called us to be. Our journeys to the shores of destiny are all different, but our mission is the same. When more of us aim to reach our destiny, we will systematically cause churches and schools to fill up, and slow the downward migration of individuals into cemeteries prematurely and correctional facilities.

The time has come for each of us to join together in love and make our father proud of his decision to place us on earth. When we reach this state of being it allows us to live and enjoy every day to the fullest. Then and only then, will we stop living for Friday and Dreading Sunday Night. God Bless You and Thank You.

Chapter 23 Questions

1. What do the shores of destiny represent to me?

_____

_____

_____

_____

2. Am I ready to begin my journey to destiny?

_____

_____

_____

_____

3. How can I help others reach their destiny?

_____

_____

_____

_____

Conclusion

Each person has the opportunity to reach and inhabit the shores of destiny within their lifetime. The goal of this book is to help assist anyone who reads it past the obstacles that may be in the way of its accomplishment. It was my aim to have the reader of this material take a look at their life, and create a plan to make the dreams of their heart become their future reality.

There are so many God given dreams that get cast aside due to the force exerted upon them by the circumstances of life. Everyone must make it through life in the best manner that their knowledge equips them to. These are not Democratic or Republican ideas in this book; they are simply God inspired recipes for dream achievement.

Reaching the shores of destiny is not an overnight or five day process from dream conception to its manifestation. It is a process that takes months and years of work. It is also a process that must be sprinkled with the perfect timing of God's favor. Everyone possesses within them the power to take control of their journey to destiny. I encourage you to take this book, its quotes and inspirational stories and let them inspire you to seek the God appointed destiny that awaits you.

The intention of this book is not to get the reader to go out and quit their job. I realize that we all have responsibilities and obligations that our jobs cover financially. To the readers that are currently unemployed, it is not a linguistical crutch to avoid finding a job to meet your current fiscally related obligations either. This book was created as a tool to enable us to examine the full reality of why we do what we do. It is a resource created to inspire individuals and let them know that no matter what their current circumstances are; their dreams are still relevant and can be achieved. Our lives are far too short to go through them unhappy with the tasks to which we devote the bulk of our time on earth to.

Over the course of our lives, most of us do not remember the first five years and forget the last ten years if we live to get old enough. What we do have is the space in between to create a life that we will remember, and the world and the loved ones we leave behind will never forget. To accomplish this task, greatness must no longer be optional for us. It must become as mandatory as death and taxes. The old motto for the US Army was "be all that you can be." It is my prayer that this book helps you to become all that God has called you to be.

There is no perfect route to the shores of destiny, but the pursuit of greatness serves as our compass. No one is perfect, but our lack of perfection should never limit our strides toward greatness. I pray that this book will bring its reader closer to God, and arms them with a plan to become functioning actors with a permanent residence at the shores of destiny.

The time has come for us to let our dreams exit our imaginations and impact the world. There are millions of books in library's and bookstores all around the world. It is no accident that this book found its way to your hands. Allow its words to stimulate your mind and let its content minister to your heart, just beside the space where the Holy Spirit of God resides. I thank you for your time, and pray that the blessings of God will overtake your life.

Key Terms

Dreams- God given maps to our destiny. They reside in our hearts adjacent to the Holy Spirit.

Purpose- The mission that God sends us to earth to fulfill. It is up to each of us to discover it during our time here. Its discovery is the chief prerequisite of destiny fulfillment.

Laboring Individuals- They are individuals that do whatever they have to in order to survive economically. They exist during the week and live for the weekend. They live with un-kept promise and unfulfilled dreams. The majority of them have not discovered their true purpose. Those that have discovered it neglect to function in it. Their steps are ordered by the call of their bills and the fluidity of their bank account. Made up of spectators and critics.

Functioning Individuals- They are individuals that have discovered their purpose for living and work within it every day. They make it a point to live every day to the fullest. They inhabit the shores of destiny. Their steps are ordered by the call of God and the desires of their heart. Made up of actors and actors emeritus.

Treasure- True wisdom imparted from one person to another.

Canvas- The circumstances we are born into or encounter in life. Its wrinkles and stains represent adversity.

Masterpiece- The portrait of our life in which the world is able to see the reflection of God's work through us.

True Human Value- Composed of the six following elements: Do we know and understand how much God loves us, How much we love and honor God, How much do we love our self, How much do we love other people, How much love we receive from other people, and How much love do we impart into our daily tasks.

Land of Security- The state of being in which we live our lives defensively instead of offensively in the pursuit of our dreams. It is inhabited by both laboring spectators and critics. It is surrounded by the sea of mediocrity. It is the state of mind in which our dreams are held captive.

Shores of Destiny- The place in which our purpose is fulfilled daily. The state of being where we honor God by using the gifts and talents that he blessed us with to serve humankind. Where the power of love and service outweighs the pull of money and social status. Its location is found at the point where our hearts, minds and the Holy Spirit of God intersect.

Bibliography

Chapter 1

Robert Kiyosaki, *The Perfect Business*, 2002, dual disc, Video Plus.

Chapter 2

Lundberg Survey, "Gas Prices skyrocket around United States" February 10, 2003. CNN (accessed Aug. 28, 2009) http://www.cnn.com/2003/US/02/09/gas.prices/index.html

AAA Fuel Data "Regular Unleaded Prices". July 2008. http://fuelgagereport.com (accessed Aug. 28 2009).

Eric Lipton, "Gramm and the Enron Loophole." The New York Times, November 17, 2008

S.O.S. Now, "Stop Oil Speculation Now-The Problem" http://stopoilspeculationnow.com/Pages/problem.aspx

Chapter 3

No Sources Used

Chapter 4

Jeremiah 1:5 NKJV

Chapter 5

Maxwell. "Lifetime." *Now*. Columbia, 2001. CD.

Chapter 6

2nd Timothy 1:6-8 NKJV

Andrew Hill and John Wooden, *Be Quick But Don't Hurry: Finding Success in the Teachings of a Lifetime*. Simon & Schuster, 2001. 156.

Chapter 7

No Sources Used

Chapter 8

Micah 7:19 NKJV

Chapter 9

Brainy Quote.com, "Abraham Lincoln Quotes," http://www.brainyquote.com/quotes/authors/a/abraham_linc oln.html(accessed Aug. 28, 2009).

Chapter 10

Matthew 6: 25-27 NKJV
John 14: 26-27 NKJV

Chapter 11

1st Timothy 6: 10 NKJV
Proverbs 18:16 NKJV
Dr. Thomas J. Stanley and Dr. William D. Danko, *The Millionaire Next Door* (New York, NY: MJF Books, 1996. 3-4.

Chapter 12

Kim Khan, "How does your debt compare?" http://moneycentral.msn.com/content/SavingandDebt/P7058 1.asp (accessed Sep. 1, 2009).
Lynnette Khalfani, *The Money Coach's Guide to Your First Million: 7 Smart Habits to Building the Wealth of Your Dreams*. (New York, NY: McGraw-Hill, 2007. 94.
Deuteronomy 28:13 NKJV
Proverbs 22:7 NKJV
James 5:16 NKJV

Matthew 17:20 NKJV
Deuteronomy 8:18 NKJV

Chapter 13

Zondra Hughes, "How Tyler Perry rose from homelessness to a $5 million dollar mansion," Ebony Magazine, January 2004,
http://findarticles.com/p/articles/mi_m1077/is_3_59/ai_1118 50312/
Michael Silver, "Holy Smokes: Rams quarterback Kurt Warner is lighting up the NFL, thanks largely to an unwavering faith that has been tested time and time again," Sports Illustrated, October 18, 1999,
http://sportsillustrated.cnn.com/vault/article/magazine/MAG 1017358/index.htm

Chapter 14
Psalms 30:5 NKJV
Proverbs 3:5 NKJV
Psalms 40:1-2 NKJV

Chapter 15
Psalms 90:10 NKJV

Chapter 16
Psalms: 37: 23-36 NKJV
Mark 12:30 NKJV
John 15:13-15 NKJV

Chapter 17
Matthew 25:37-40 NKJV
Matthew 6:24 NKJV
Ezekiel 36:26-27 NKJV
John 14:26 NKJV
Romans 14:12-13 NKJV
John 14:15-17 NKJV
John 14:6 NKJV

Chapter 18

Psalms 55:22 NKJV
Habakkuk 2:1-2 NKJV

Chapter 19

Acts 17:26-27 NKJV
Malachi 3:8 NKJV

Chapter 20

Isaiah 43:18-19 NKJV
Here Come The Judges: "TV jury rules in favor of charismatic decision makers." Ebony Magazine, May 2002

Oprah Winfrey Biography, bio. True Story
http://www.biography.com/articles/Oprah-Winfrey-9534419?part=0

Laura Sternberg, "Eminem's Detroit Roots: The Detroit Background of Marshall Bruce Mathers III" March 28, 2008, http://detroit.about.com/od/peoplelifestyles/a/Eminem.htm (accessed Sep, 28, 2009.)
Jia Lynn Yang, "Happyness for sale: He's gone from single dad to successful stockbroker. And that's just the start for Chris Gardner Inc.," September 15, 2006 (http://money.cnn.com/magazines/fortune/fortune_archive/2006/09/18/8386184/index.htm (accessed Nov. 15, 2006.)

Ron Lewis, "Bernard Hopkins credits time in prison with shaping his legend." Times Online, April 18, 2008, http://www.timesonline.co.uk/tol/sport/more_sport/article3767474.ece (accessed Oct. 1, 2009.)

Sylvester Stallone, Origin of Rocky Balboa Total Rocky: The Ultimate guide to the Rocky movies http://www.totalrocky.com/films/rocky/production.shtml (accessed Jan. 1, 2007.)

Chapter 21

Nielsen A2/M2 Three Screen Report 4th quarter 2008, "TV, Internet and Mobile Usage In U.S. Continues To Rise." February 23, 2009, http://blog.nielsen.com/nielsenwire/online_mobile/tv-internet-and-mobile-usage-in-us-continues-to-rise/

Mega Millions "More Than 2.4 Million Tickets Win as Mega Millions Jackpot Grows To $325 Million." August 26, 2009. http://www.megamillions.com/mcenter/pressrelease.asp?newsID=ECA1A3A0-E6C5-4187-9BC1-E21010000624

Powerball- Prizes and Odds
http://www.powerball.com/powerball/pb_prizes.asp

Chapter 22

1.1[st] Corinthians 7:22-24 NKJV

Chapter 23

1.1[st] Corinthians 12:4-7 NKJV
2.Matthew 6:33 NKJV
3.Ephesians 4:7-8 NKJV
4.1[st] Corinthians 13:1-3 NKJV

CPSIA information can be obtained at www.ICGtesting.com
Printed in the USA
BVOW04s0257200215

388554BV00006B/81/P